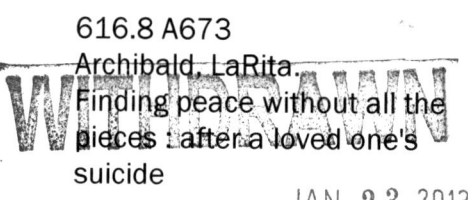
"Oh, how I wish *Finding Peace Without All The Pieces* had been available when our sons died. LaRita Archibald is truly a pioneer in the area of suicide bereavement, and her book gives survivors the resources and tools to keep living one step at a time. Her tragic story is interwoven among other heartbreaking stories, but with every chapter LaRita's strength and character shine through as a beacon of light and hope. She courageously addresses head on the stigma in religion and our culture that has kept the topic of mental illness and death by suicide relegated to the darkest corners of society and has left surviving families, both civilian and military, living out their lives under clouds of fear, shame, guilt, and abandonment. It is my honor to wholeheartedly recommend this book to anyone who has lost someone to suicide. LaRita writes her story the way she lives her life, with true compassion born out of her own broken heart and her deepest desire to lovingly bring knowledge, understanding, enlightenment and healing to ultimately save lives in memory of her own precious son."

> — *Carol Graham, wife of Major General Mark Graham, who lost one son to suicide and the other to the war in Iraq*

D1554629

FINDING PEACE
WITHOUT
ALL THE PIECES

AFTER A LOVED ONE'S SUICIDE

 හැඕ

LaRita Archibald

ISBN-13 978-0615611860

Larch Publishing
www.larchpublishing.com
Colorado Springs, CO

Printed in the United States of America
First Printing March 2012

Designed by Megan Herndon

In loving memory of my son, Roger Kent Archibald,
who lived from August 22, 1954 to August 30, 1978.
He was a fun and funny, generous, loving, kind and gentle man
deeply loved by his family.
The world is greatly diminished without him.

This book is dedicated to

my husband, Eldon, who shared my heartbreak and
encouraged me in how I chose to give it meaning,

our children . . . my inspiration: sons, Craig, Curtis, and Kevin
and daughter, Karen, who gave me strength, laughter, hope and
the delight of nine grandchildren,

all the others who left too soon,

and, especially, those who mourn their leaving.

CONTENTS

Foreword — 1

Acknowledgments — 5

A Mite of Understanding — 7

Dear Bereaved Friends — 11

PERSONAL PIECES

The First Day of Forever — 15

And Forever More — 19

Astray in a Foreign Land — 25

A Family Retreat — 29

The Family's Survival — 31

EMPOWERING PIECES

About Suicide — 37

About Grief — 39

Not All Loss Through Death Is the Same — 45

Not All Grief Is the Same — 55

Not All Grief After Suicide Is the Same — 61

Suicide Grief Strata — 73

Shame, Silence, and Stigma — 77

Striving to Understand Depression — 81

ENLIGHTENING PIECES

Coping on a Different Psychological Level   87

Is Suicide a Choice?   93

Is Suicide a Selfish and Cowardly Act?   97

Religious Reflections on Suicide   101

Phantom Pain   107

Flashbacks   111

Children Bereaved by Suicide   115

Grandparent Grief   123

Survivors of Military Suicide   127

PRACTICAL PIECES

Assuming or Assigning Blame   139

Closure and Recovery   141

Deeds of Omission and Commission   145

To Move or Not to Move   151

Life Insurance   157

Marital Intimacy   167

About Divorce   171

Surrogate Parenting   173

MISSING PIECES

Bits and Pieces   179

Searching for Answers   183

The Obsessive Review   185

PEACE

Self Care 191

Forgiveness 195

Mourning Tasks of Suicide Bereaved 197

Taking Charge of Mourning 201

Victim ~ Survivor ~ Thriver 205

A Peaceful Plateau 209

APPENDICES

Survivor Resources 213

To the Newly Bereaved After Suicide 215

Posttraumatic Stress Disorder After Suicide 219

Putting Responsibility into Perspective 221

Heavy Hearts During Holidays 223

Helping Survivors After Suicide 225

A Suicide Survivor's Beatitudes 229

FOREWORD

I first met LaRita in the receiving line of a funeral I had officiated at. She was a beautiful woman with the most compassionate eyes I had ever seen. She paused, and asked about my non-profit, First Steps Spirituality Center, which provides spiritual support for hurting children and teens. She asked if I had had much experience working with children or teens who had survived the suicide of a parent or sibling. I told her that I had limited experience but was glad to see any children she might send my way. She smiled a warm smile and then asked if she could meet with me.

I had met with many professionals in our community and thought I was prepared for the meeting with LaRita. I expected her to ask me the usual questions about number of visits for each child and cost of the program. Instead she asked me several questions about how I would be meeting the needs of her children, the ones she would send me, who had survived suicide. She asked if I knew the difference between a person grieving a suicide and someone grieving another kind of death. She asked my theological position about suicide and how I would answer a child wanting to know if the church condemned suicide.

By the end of our visit, I had no idea if LaRita would ever refer a child to my center, but I was certain that this woman knew more about suicide than anyone I had ever spoken to and that I wanted to learn all I could from her. This began our fourteen-year affiliation as colleagues who deeply care about those who suffer loss. She became my trusted friend, and soon my teacher and counselor.

Only two years later, my nephew completed suicide. I called LaRita, attended her support group, and received her care. Her compassion and her expertise helped my entire family through the worst nightmare of our lives.

There are many ways to become an authority on a topic. Some read lots of books, study hard, and learn in an academic manner. LaRita has read everything, I think, that has been written about suicide and has studied extensively. However, that is not what has made LaRita an expert.

LaRita became an expert because, when her son died from a self-inflicted gunshot wound, she searched for an authority to help her, to guide her, and to educate her and could find no one. She had to educate herself. She read, studied, and began Heartbeat, a support group for others grieving suicide loss.

She has not only read books and articles, but through deep, compassionate, and non-judgmental listening, she has learned how people grieve when someone they love completes suicide, what unique challenges they face, what is most and least helpful, and what best helps them survive the loss and eventually learn to live again.

LaRita did not choose to be an authority on this painful topic. She does not look like an authority; she looks more like a sweet, unassuming mother. She does not act like an authority; she is humble. She is not a hardened academic; she still meets with compassion every person who needs her help. But she is an authority on how to survive the aftermath of suicide.

Listening to LaRita speak at many events and support groups has helped me understand and minister to the hurting children, teens, and families that now come to First Steps for help. I am confident because I have been taught by one who truly knows, from every angle, about the impact of suicide on those who lose a loved one to it.

Like so many of those whose lives she has touched, I have been encouraging her to write this book for a very long time. *Finding Peace Without All The Pieces* is a beautiful mixture of practical advice and personal experiences offering hope that learning to live again after a suicide touches one's life is possible. The book is written in short, easy-to-read chapters so that even someone in acute grief will be able to digest it. I highly recommend it to anyone who has been touched by the death of a friend, family member, or coworker who completed suicide. There is not a better book to guide them through their time of grief. It is also a must read for professionals such as pastors, teachers, mental health workers, students, and medical professionals. After reading this book, you will be equipped to assist those who are grieving with confidence and sensitivity.

LaRita tells me that "suicide is its own unique grief." From my personal experiences and from working with families who have been touched by suicide, I believe her words are true. There is much about a person ending his or her life that intensifies the pain and makes the questioning deeper than with other losses.

If you have lost a loved one to suicide, I know this book will help you. Read it and know that it was written to bring you the information you need and the comfort you so desperately seek.

If you are a professional, I urge you to read this book so that when suicide affects someone in your life, you will be prepared to meet their needs in the best way possible.

I am so sorry that LaRita has had to endure the pain she has experienced since the loss of her son, but I am grateful that she has taken that tragedy and brought from it the gift that this book is. Because of her determination never to let another person endure what she did without support, she has created this book. I am confident that it will heal and bring hope to the people who need it.

I am beyond grateful to LaRita for being my friend, mentor, teacher, support, and now for writing this book. Thank you, my friend and bless you for sharing all that you have with others!

— Rev. Dr. Leanne Hadley, President and Founder,
First Steps Spirituality Center

ACKNOWLEDGMENTS

Every tragedy, every tear shared with me by survivors of suicide loss is represented in some way in this book. You have taught me the true meaning of strength, resiliency and courage. I am especially grateful to those who trusted me to write of their broken hearts and their struggle to regain joy in living. I believe nothing we endure in life is wasted if we make something good from it. Your struggles offer hope and your tears are a soothing balm to others who must travel this bitter road.

I thank my beloved parents, my brothers, extended family, and dear friends for listening, for loving, supporting, and encouraging me. It would have been an impossibly brutal and desolate journey without you.

And special thanks to Michelle, Leanne, and many others who told me "you must write a book", then were persistent in their inquiry of its progress until it was done.

A Mite of Understanding

I groped along grief's bitter road, rent by sorrow and despair.
Fear of empty days ahead seemed more than I could bear.
The throbbing of each heartbeat was an act of agony.
Relentless questions in my mind fought to torture me.
I relived unhappy moments, each conflict I retraced.
I examined every action, invading each private space.
Oh! I searched so hard for answers to know the reason why
when he had the choice to live, my son would choose to die.

Wracked by smothering anguish for his death's futility,
I cried in desolation for the touch of empathy.
But I found myself an alien, astray in a foreign land,
suddenly speaking language no one could understand.

I felt the arms of friendship. I saw others turn away.
I heard the judging of my child by things that people say.
I became obsessed with anger, with a need to fault and blame.
I felt the whip of stigma; tasted the bitter gall of shame.

I felt soul-searing torment for whatever part I'd played
in the depletion of self-love whence his choice was made.
I viewed myself a failure. His act diminished me.
For I somehow should have known, been able to foresee.

I felt deep, sharp rejection, assaulted by his choice.
I tried to think his thoughts; the reasons he would voice.

All the while I'm searching; so confusing is the quest,
for a mite of understanding to put my pain to rest.

Yet, could I see his face again and if my arms could hold,
would I accept his reasons if this is what he told?

"Mother, please forgive me, but I couldn't stop to weigh
the price my desperate choice would leave for you to pay.
Once I had golden dreams of the promise life held for me
and I reached with eager hands to grasp their certainty.
I reached to find fulfillment, to know my place on earth.
I reached to find achievement, to reinforce my worth.
I looked to find a purpose to assure my dignity.
I sought to find the strength to thwart adversity.
I reached to find the wisdom my faltering steps to guide.
I sought to find the courage to walk the paths untried.

I reached to find the discipline to lift me toward my goal.
I prayed to keep the faith to bind my wounded soul.
I longed to find compassion for the injuries of the climb.
I tried to have the patience to give my dreams more time.
I looked from all directions to see my life worthwhile,
But I found so many viewpoints that ended in denial.

Fear and doubt assailed me, their ghostly shadows haunting;
efforts seemed doomed to failure, mistakes forever taunting.
I felt so trapped and helpless. I lost the strength to cope.
The future loomed dark and vast, lonely ... cold ... void of hope.

Then, spent by the pain within me and its pounding for release,
I sought a place to rest awhile, to find a moment's peace.

Please forgive me, Mother, and know these words are true:
I did not make this choice from lack of loving you."

I screamed my blinded rage at God for deserting my son and me.
"How could You let this happen? allow this choice to be?"
Then I felt His love enfold me; this truth my faith renew;
God never makes mistakes, but His children often do.

"I hate your futile choice, my child. I doubt it was your right,
for you took the peace of others with you in your flight.
I have some understanding now, though it doesn't dry my tears,
it doesn't fill my empty arms or replace your wasted years.
But I know God accepted you. He knew your desolate cry.
And as He extends forgiveness, son, then surely, so can I."

I mourn the loss of dimpled smiles, of gentle deed and merry wit.
His choice becomes my life ... in part, but never the whole of it!
For I, too, have a choice to make. Endless grieving will not serve.
I'll accept the peace of mind I know that I deserve.
So I've put aside my searching, my quest for reasons why,
for reasons will not comfort me, nor answers satisfy.
I've cast aside self-pity's shroud, forged the hell of black despair.
I've turned my eyes toward future's plain and hope of joy
   awaiting there.

Yes! I've gained some understanding. Oh, how harshly it was
earned!

But I've also gained the strength to use what I have learned;

to give the touch of empathy when it's solace others seek,

to lend a listening heart when this grief has need to speak.

For I have learned of those who know this wound I feel,

and by sharing the pain of others, I help my own to heal.

So if you must walk my bitter road, your tears mingle with
my own,

find some comfort knowing, friend, you do not walk alone.

LaRita Archibald©, 1983

Dear Bereaved Friends:

Finding Peace Without All The Pieces: After a Loved One's Suicide offers suicide bereaved and their caregivers what was not available to me after my son ended his life in 1978: assurance that suicide loss is survivable, that you won't always hurt as badly as you do today, and that there will be a time when you will again flourish and feel joy in living.

My objective in writing this book is to comfort, encourage, and offer hope. I share scenarios that may be abrasive and painful to survivors whose suicide loss is new and raw. Although I believe every page is important, I urge you to postpone reading any chapter you find hurtful until you are stronger.

The poem *A Mite of Understanding* summarizes my grief journey to some degree. It was written early in my mourning as I struggled to piece together my son's need to be free, my need to understand his pain, and my emotional responses and reconciliation to his death. Perhaps it will provide other suicide bereaved a bit of solace.

The section entitled *Personal Pieces* describes some of the trauma my family experienced in the early hours and days following my son's death. It is my wish that you will be empowered knowing others have seen the face of suicide, endured the anguish of suicide loss, and worked through that terrible mire of pain to grow strong and know peace again.

Enlightening Pieces, Practical Pieces, and *Empowering Pieces* define some of the complexities of grief after suicide and how other suicide bereaved work through the pain of their tragedies toward a peaceful plateau. Several chapters describe extreme circumstances suicide bereaved have faced, adapted to, reconciled with, and live beyond. I am deeply grateful to all who generously extended encouragement to readers by sharing how they coped with unimaginably painful situations. They exemplify the indomitable strength of the human spirit.

Missing Pieces are my effort to normalize the suicide grief process, to correct some myths about suicide that unnecessarily complicate our grief journey.

Peace extends the promise that acute grief eventually subsides and that, as we mourn, the healing we achieve allows us to look toward the future, to feel joy and a revived love of being alive.

The appendices are articles written during thirty years of sharing with suicide bereaved that many have found helpful. Permission to use *A Suicide Survivor's Beatitudes* at memorial or funeral services after a suicide is frequently requested. This piece may be used as printed, referencing my authorship, without my permission, in whatever manner gives comfort to suicide bereaved and help to those who support them.

Take what you need from these pages, my wounded friend; use them for your strengthening and healing. Try to find some comfort in knowing you are not alone. There are others who know your anguish.

With love and understanding,

- LaRita

PERSONAL PIECES

The First Day of Forever

"What the caterpillar calls the end of the world,
the Master calls the butterfly."

Richard Bach, *Illusions*

In the wee hours of the morning of August 30, 1978, the serenity of my snug, family-focused life was shattered by what sounded like a door slamming. My husband, Eldon, found our twenty-four-year-old son, Kent, lying on our family room floor, breathing laboriously, mortally wounded by a self-inflicted shotgun wound to his abdomen. In an instant our world had exploded into a hellish nightmare to be succeeded by smothering anguish, confusing angers, and an agonizing sense of guilt and responsibility; an alien, isolated world that reverberated with incessant echoes of why. Why had this happened? Why hadn't we known? How could suicide happen in our family?

Eldon's first response to finding our gut-shot son lying on the floor was to lift the shotgun from across his midsection, eject the shell, and take the gun to its usual place in the furnace room.

I knelt by Kent's side, told him I loved him and what a special part of our family he was. I took great care not to chastise, for I recalled one's hearing was the last sense to go and, instinctively, I knew the remainder of his life was measured in minutes. I seemed to float on the ceiling, looking down upon myself and my dying son. I saw my fingers reach out and trace tear stains on his cheeks. Knowing his deep love for his family I saw his tears as reflections of his anguish at leaving us. All the while, in the background, I heard a terrible mewing sound like a wounded animal caught in a trap. It was my own keening.

The arriving ambulance blared our tragedy to the world. Four police cars pulled in front of our home. Six or seven officers swarmed through our front door. Without a word of acknowledgment or concern for my husband, me, our nineteen-year-old son, Curtis, or my visiting parents, they set about their investigation. As Eldon, Curtis, and I moved to follow the ambulance that carried our dying child and brother to the hospital, an officer grasped my husband's arm and informed him he would not be permitted to leave. He was needed to answer questions. Urging us on, Eldon promised to follow immediately. I wanted to ride in the ambulance with Kent but I feared being in the way and the moment to ask passed instantly.

Curtis and I drove to the small local hospital and ran to the emergency room door. It was locked. I pounded to be admitted. The night watchman moved slowly to unlock it and reprimanded me for creating a disturbance. The glaring waiting room was sterile and empty. None of the limited night staff could be spared from this emergency to respond to our anxious concerns. There were no pastoral personnel to offer prayer or consolation, seek information, or help in making calls to my other children. I could not comprehend the questions on the forms that had been shoved into my hands. As I sat facing the clock I watched a nurse's interminable struggle to pull a ponderous machine up the hall and into the room where my son lay. I wanted to scream at her to hurry. Hurry!

Twenty minutes passed and Eldon had not arrived. I called home urging him to come. More time passed. Again I called home. A police officer answered and crisply informed me my husband would be delayed. I pleaded that he be allowed to come immediately, explaining that our son was dying. The third time I called, Eldon answered in a voice I scarcely recognized. He said, "They think I did it! They think I shot Kent!" They accused him, I later learned, of having a quarrel with our son and in his rage, picking up the shotgun, shoving it into Kent's belly, and pulling the trigger. All the while Eldon protested, "No, No, that's not the way it was," and my parents confirmed his denial.

Finally, the note my son had written was discovered tilted against the wall of the family room, where it had come to rest during the flurry of activity. Satisfied at last that Kent's injury had, in fact, been self-inflicted, the police gathered their clipboards and investigative paraphernalia and departed. They left my elderly parents alone without the comfort of a neighbor or a family member. They left Eldon to drive alone to the hospital, where he fell into my arms when I told him Kent had died.

The doctor and nurses were gentle as they told me what I had known from the beginning: the injury Kent had inflicted upon himself was beyond repair. The .12-gauge shotgun blast to his abdomen had destroyed nearly every vital organ. Even had they been able to keep him alive, his future would have been a torment of partially functioning organs, inestimable pain, and dependency upon a full-time care provider.

I wanted to go to him, to kiss his face, to smooth his hair, to tell him once again how much I loved him, and to give him permission to be at peace. I wanted to touch him while his body was still warm and familiar and my own. I had seen what he had done to his body. I needed to see what they had done to make him comfortable in his dying. My request was either unheard or deliberately ignored, for I was not allowed to be with him. Fear of breaching propriety kept me from insisting. The lost opportunity to hold him one last time, to tell him how much he was loved, has left a permanent void in my mourning.

I was handed a telephone book, opened to the yellow pages, and told I must choose a mortuary.

And Forever More

*"Life will not go in the same way without him.
The fact that he left behind a place that cannot be filled
is a high tribute to the uniqueness of his soul."*

Molly Fumis, *Safe Passages*

The sun was rising as my husband and I drove home from the hospital in silence, each trapped in the horror of what had taken place. I wanted to reach across the seat and touch him, but my hand was leaden, immobile. At the same time my mind raced, hopscotching in short, disconnected thoughts. Our beautiful family was shattered forever. How could we live with that? Would Curtis be permanently scarred by the horror of seeing his gut-shot brother? How would we tell Craig and Kevin, Kent's oldest and youngest brothers, of his death? How would his death affect the new marriage of our daughter, Karen, Kent's close friend and confidante? How could we tell his grandparents this beloved grandson had deliberately ended his life? How could we tell our friends? How would they look at our family? What would they think of Kent??

I felt a tremendous need to protect him from curious, prying minds, from judgment and whatever might be said. Simultaneously, I was filled with rage at what he had done to himself and to our family. This could not have happened! Surely I would awaken and find it was all a ghastly nightmare.

My husband, usually a take-charge guy, sat unresponsive, nearly catatonic from the emotional flogging he had suffered and unable to participate in immediate decision making. I was just the opposite, in a frenetic state, needing to take action, to regain some control. The mortician's call about embalming prompted me to focus on funeral plans. I began deciding upon pallbearers, noting favorite scripture, selecting music, considering soloists and who would perform the funeral service. I selected clothes to take to the mortuary and started writing Kent's obituary. My youngest brother, a Denver attorney and former army mortuary officer, telephoned his offer to help. I told him I could handle things. I felt that since it was our family's problem, we should be the ones to take care of it. Much later I realized how cruel my rejection of his offer was. In truth, I had no idea what needed to be done. His caring presence and expertise would have spared my family emotional energy, mistakes, and regret.

In my early religious education I had been taught that those who usurped God's wisdom and power by ending their lives were condemned to spend eternity in the fiery furnaces of hell. This belief had lain dormant, to erupt that day into a monstrous, clutching entanglement of doubt that placed me in immediate conflict with my understanding of a merciful God.

I could not believe that my Loving God would slam the gates of Heaven in the face of my child. I turned to the clergy who visited us late in the forenoon. One ministered in the church we had most recently attended; the other was a new minister in the church where my family had worshiped for more than twenty-five years, where our children had been baptized, educated, and confirmed. I expected compassion, comfort, and direction. I pleaded for relief for my concerns for the repose of my son's soul. Their rigid beliefs did not allow them to offer it. Instead, they quoted scripture and platitudes that seemed to reinforce a judgmental, condemning God, a God who would, indeed, separate my son from his family throughout eternity. They avoided mentioning the manner of my son's death and suggested we put it quickly and quietly behind us.

I was totally bereft. These clergy left me this choice: I could repudiate God, their harsh, denying God, or I could rely upon my own, by then wavering, faith in an all-caring, all-forgiving Almighty. At that time, to believe in God at all I had to believe He had known and understood my son's pain-filled state of mind, had sorrowed for his choice, but forgave the choice he made and offered him Eternal Peace. It took many months of searching through dogma and doctrine to resolve this dimension of my grief and to reaffirm my "God of love."

We began making burial arrangements before two of our sons arrived home from Michigan where the youngest, fourteen-year-old Kevin, was visiting his oldest brother, Craig, a Michigan state employee. We had no previous plan for which of the four local cemeteries would be chosen for the burial of family members. We finally opted for a perpetual care cemetery where Kent's aunt and uncle owned plots. It seemed important that he not be alone.

We had made an appointment, but when we arrived at the cemetery office, no one was there to greet us. We seated ourselves in the public waiting room, our anguish in full view of all who passed. After a time we were approached by a man I mistook for a cemetery workman. He wore a food-spotted tie, shirtsleeves rolled up, trousers rumpled, and a large collection of keys hanging from his belt that he jangled incessantly. He introduced himself as a funeral director and ushered us into his office. He asked how our son had died and responded to our answer with a flustered laugh. He asked if Kent had been on drugs and when we shook our heads 'no,' his comment was, "Well, his life must have been terrible for him to want to die."

We told the director we wanted to purchase eight lots to accommodate the eventual needs of the entire family. He unrolled a large map and proceeded to show us available lots. The telephone rang. The caller obviously was a golfing friend. They spoke briefly about a golf date before he excused himself, explaining that he was with clients whose son had killed himself. I was devastated by his disparaging attitude, at being reduced from a heartbroken family to "clients," without dignity, feeling, or hearing, unworthy of compassion or courtesy and without the strength or courage to protest.

After selecting lots from the cemetery map, my husband and I were ushered into the director's car to drive to the grave sites while our daughter, Karen, her husband, and our son, Curtis, waited in the cemetery office. Seated facing the director's desk, Karen had distractedly reached to touch a small, black, oblong box lying on the desk in front of her. The lid flew open and a tiny skeleton popped out and danced insanely before their eyes. We returned to the cemetery office to find our grown children laughing and crying hysterically.

The director advised us that a sizable deposit was necessary to reserve the selected lots and that before our son's grave could be opened, full payment for his lot was required. As we moved to sign the contract presented to us, the director discovered that some of the lots we had chosen were already sold. Again he unrolled the map and showed us other available sites. This time he took us to the window and pointed in the general direction of the new lots, leaving my husband and me to stumble amidst others' graves to acquaint ourselves with our son's final resting place.[1]

As we were driven to the Denver airport to pick up our sons in the late afternoon I felt ill, as if I were suffering the onset of the flu. My head throbbed, my body ached, my heart raced, my voice was hoarse, my throat sore, and I was chilled despite the

---

[1] *Late one evening, about ten days following Kent's funeral, I answered a telephone call from a woman identifying herself as the wife of a gravedigger in the cemetery where our son was buried. She asked if we were aware that cemetery site was a reclaimed natural lakebed and that there was two feet of water in Kent's grave at the time of his burial. Upon verification of this extremely disturbing information we decided to move Kent to another cemetery. The move was completed with the help of a mortician friend who filed appropriate paperwork and authorization from my attorney brother to the cemetery for release of his body. The short-term emotional and financial expense was much the same as the original burial; the long-term peace of mind, priceless.*

heat of the August evening. "This is no time for me to be sick," I thought, not knowing physical symptoms often accompany acute bereavement.

We reviewed with Craig and Kevin the events surrounding Kent's death, answering questions and comforting them as best we could. When I shared the plans for Kent's service, Craig said, "Mother, there is nothing left for us to do. He's our brother. We need to carry Kent to his grave." My well-intended effort to protect my children from the emotional burden of making funeral arrangements had nearly deprived them of the privilege and their right to participate in the ritual of their brothers' burial. It was an error that could be corrected. Kent's three brothers, two cousins and our daughter's husband would serve as his pallbearers.

I fell into bed that first night, exhausted. My mother tucked me in and kissed me goodnight as she had when I was a small child. Before I fell asleep, blessedly unaware of the torment-filled months that lay ahead, I thanked God that this terrible day was finally over.

Astray in a Foreign Land

*"I found myself an alien, astray in a foreign land,
suddenly speaking language no one could understand."*

LaRita Archibald, *A Mite of Understanding*

Our friends and family surrounded us with love and sympathy. There were those who shared with us their understanding of the hopes and dreams lost when a child dies. But there was none who had had the experience of being robbed of those hopes and dreams because their child had deliberately caused his own death.

There was no one to validate our feelings or encourage us to voice the horror of seeing the mutilation our son had inflicted upon himself. There was no one to guide us through the great morass of emotional turmoil, to role-model healthy resolution of suicide loss, or to extend the encouragement that we would not always hurt this badly. There was no one to put their arms around us and offer the solace of, *"I know your anguish, I've been there."*

We were adrift in a sea of despair and relentless, tormenting questions. What had hurt this young man so badly he wanted to die? Why hadn't we known the extent and depth of his pain? Why hadn't he told us? We would have helped him! Surely we could have prevented his death! And what is the nature of a mother who feels more shock and disbelief for the fact that her son has killed himself than for the fact he is dead? What distorted thinking causes her to wish his death had been from any other cause? And why, because he created his own death, implying he wanted to be dead, does she question her right to grieve?

I felt soiled and separated, even from my brothers and my parents. For the first time in my life, I was embarrassed for myself, for my family, and for my dead son. So much of what I had always believed about suicide was contradicted by my son's life and his death. He was intelligent, handsome, creative, and witty; gentle, caring, generous, and deeply loved by his family. My feelings of estrangement from my social community were relieved to some extent by a comment from a long time friend, a civic leader, when he called upon us and said, "My God! If this can happen in your family, it could happen to any of us."

Nothing I had previously learned or experienced of grief prepared me for the smothering, heart-piercing anguish I suffered. A counselor I visited told me, "The death of a child is the death of a child . . . you are feeling the pain and loss all parents feel after a child dies." Instinctively I knew that how one's child dies impacts the grieving, that there were grief dynamics following suicide not present in bereavement from other causes of death. The counselor's lack of understanding of this reality caused me to despair of professional help.

Less than a week after Kent's funeral I was at the library searching for answers and ways to help myself and my family. What I found that day wasn't comforting. I learned from Albert Cain's book *Survivors of Suicide* that we had an identity, that those left to mourn were called *survivors of suicide* and *survivor-victims*. Somewhere in my searching I read that those left behind after an immediate family member's deliberately self-inflicted death were at greater risk of eventually ending their lives. This added tremendous fear to my grief. Was I to lose another child in this manner? Or my husband? Was it possible that I, in a moment weakened by despair, would lose control and end my life?

Could I survive the intensity of my pain? Did I want to? I was driven by a frantic sense of urgency to separate and define what

I was feeling. I was convinced that if I could gain some understanding of the bewildering chaos of grief, rather than feeling disoriented and overwhelmed, I would be strengthened with a measure of control that would enable me to better manage my jumbled morass of anguish. I needed to know why I felt such guilt and a sense of unmet responsibility when my entire motherhood had been focused on guiding healthy, stable children to adulthood. How had we so failed this son? What had we done or not done? Why was I so angry at myself, at God, sometimes at other family members and, perhaps most painful of all, at my dead son? I was obsessed with the need to know why my son had killed himself.

A Family Retreat

"There are two parties to the suffering that death inflicts;
and in the apportionment of this suffering, the survivor
takes the brunt."

Arnold Toynbee, *Man's Concern with Death*

We can see Pikes Peak from our living room. Our family loved spending time in the mountains skiing, fishing, hiking, rafting, camping, and horseback riding. In anticipation of our oldest son's late summer visit, we had reserved a cabin on the Gunnison River for a family getaway over the Labor Day weekend. We all were looking forward to it . . . my husband and I, our four sons, including Kent, and our daughter, Karen, and her husband.

Kent died early Wednesday morning. His funeral was Friday afternoon before Labor Day weekend. Saturday morning my parents packed us into our car insisting we keep our mountain cabin reservation. We were numb, limp and puppet-like, totally uninterested; it didn't matter one way or another. For three long days we had struggled with the horror of suicide, made painful decisions, fielded questions, poured gallons of coffee, answered phone calls and accepted hugs, casseroles, and floral arrangements. We had been constantly surrounded by people who came to offer condolences, who wanted us to know they were there for us. We were overwhelmed and exhausted by all that had taken place. We needed quiet time. My parents recognized the need for our shattered family to be alone.

The weekend was not the fun, carefree time we had planned early in the summer, but it served an invaluable purpose. We talked and talked and found that each of us had a different view of why Kent had ended his life and that none of us really knew. Each family member expressed concern for the others and found some relief, with all promising that if they needed help they would tell another.

We hiked until we were tired, then sat down on the forest trails, talked some more, and cried together. At night we sat around a campfire, reminiscing about past times . . . most good, some not so much. We had some chuckles and tears, and we had prayer and tears. We took a river raft trip but the river was so low our guide asked us to get out of the raft and carry it over the rocks to deeper water. We slipped and slid, got very wet, and laughed and cried some more. Somehow that raft trip was symbolic of the journey that lay ahead.

This time our broken family had alone was an unexpected gift. It allowed us to share our feelings within the private shelter of those we were closest to. It reassured each of us that we would somehow endure the pain of Kent's death and that in time we would be strong again. Most importantly, it provided an opportunity to re-bond as a family, with one forever missing. They were bittersweet days of sorrow, tenderness, and solidarity that provided us all assurance that we would survive and provided me a focus in the following weeks and months when the horror of the night Kent killed himself would replay in my mind.

The Family's Survival

*"The family is not linear; it is a circular unit
in which what each person does affects the other members
of the unit."*

Michelle Linn-Gust, *Rocky Roads*

The family structure constantly shifts and changes. When one member is absent the structure is out of balance and must adjust to right itself. I doubt anything causes greater change, shift, challenge, or adjustment in a family than the suicide of one of its own.

For some time, coping after Kent's suicide felt like crawling through a briar patch in the dark, without guidance or direction. All the anguished family members struggled to find their way; confused and fearful of wrong turns and pitfalls, retracing steps, guarding against re-injury, extending a helping hand to one another when they had the strength and presence of mind to do so; all the while each looking for, hoping for an easier, safer, less painful way through the maze of grief and into the sunlight. Each member survived the journey differently; all scarred, toughened, and changed, but still closely knit, united: a family.

The day our son and brother ended his life our family added *suicide* to its vocabulary. Before that day, the word had a vague and distant meaning not applicable to us, a word rarely thought or spoken and never a topic of family conversation. After Kent's death the word *suicide* seemed to be everywhere. It thrust itself boldly from newspapers and spoke brazenly from the television. My ears developed *suicide* antenna that pick up the word a block away. It was not a word that could be silenced, hidden, or ignored. Kent's act made suicide a family affair. In word and deed, suicide became part of our everyday life. Our family chose to give the word benefit, purpose, and meaning, with every family member, in their own way, contributing to that result.

Propelled by isolation and lack of genuine empathy or validation for grief following suicide loss, I was determined to provide a setting where those bereaved by suicide could gather and help one another. In 1980, I started HEARTBEAT, among the first suicide bereavement support groups formed anywhere. My husband agreed to help me, although he expressed concern for my disappointment if no one came. Not only did people come but within a few months other communities and states asked to form chapters, and one of the first guidelines for suicide grief support groups was written. My husband encouraged me, supported the effort financially, and attended nearly every meeting for almost ten years. Curtis, Kent's younger brother, served as leader of the sibling survivors.

Our youngest son, Kevin, a high school student, told me, "Mom, if you're going to do something, do it for the kids." I had learned teens were a high-risk age group, and we developed a suicide awareness classroom presentation that was in frequent demand by high school health teachers. I joined forces with others in my state concerned with the high suicide rate to form a statewide suicide prevention organization focused primarily on providing awareness in schools.

My daughter was my sounding board and critic, reading and suggesting and encouraging. Our oldest son, by then working toward an MBA at an eastern university, was a long-distance consultant and cheerleader. In 1995, my daughter's son, sixteen-year-old Timothy, represented youth as a director on the board of the Suicide Prevention Partnership of the Pikes Peak Region, an organization I co-founded specifically to address suicide as a preventable health problem in my community.

Our nine grandchildren entered a family where *suicide* was spoken without reservation but discriminately, with respect and awareness of its meaning and power. I wanted them to view suicide as a preventable tragedy, never as an option. At some time, as they have grown into young adults, every grandchild has sought advice concerning a friend and has learned how to respond and where to get help. Each has written a paper or made informed class presentations on the subject of suicide, advancing suicide awareness for themselves and among their peers.

There is no immunity to suicide but there is information that offers protection when suicide is seen as an option. I am comfortable knowing my family is equipped with knowledge about suicide and would seek mental health help if or when they need it.

With confidence, and no small amount of relief, I believe my children dealt with their brother's death as well as I could have hoped. They all have children of their own and busy, productive lives. My husband and I continue a loving relationship. We enjoy good health and as many good times as advancing years allow. Life holds joy for us again.

EMPOWERING PIECES

About Suicide

*"Your pain is the breaking of the shell
that encloses your understanding."*

Khalil Gibran, *The Prophet*

In his book *The Suicidal Mind*, Edwin S. Shneidman defines Ten Commonalities of Suicide. These commonalities offered me a foundation for what I so desperately needed: some understanding of my son's state of mind before he ended his life. The commonalities I found most useful are these.

1. The common purpose of suicide is to seek a solution, a way out of a problem, a dilemma, a difficulty, a crisis, an unbearable situation that is generating intense suffering. We may never know what that problem or situation was. Even if we knew, we wouldn't agree that it was bad enough to die for.

2. The common goal of suicide is cessation of consciousness to stop the unendurable pain. The moment the possibility that stopping consciousness will stop the pain occurs, the scenario for suicide begins.

3. The common stimulus of suicide is unbearable psychological pain. Pain is the core of suicide. The individual perceives the pain as intolerable and unending. Dr. Shneidman describes the psychological pain as psychache.

4. The common stressor in suicide is frustrated psychological needs. Suicide stems from thwarted, blocked or unfulfilled psychological needs that cause the pain and the push for release, escape.

5. The common emotion in suicide is hopelessness-helplessness. The despondent mind-set that 'nothing I can do will change what I need to have changed in order to be free of the pain' renders the individual unable to act to help himself or herself.

Why People Die By Suicide, by Thomas Joiner, Bright-Burton Professor of Psychology at Florida State University and survivor of his father's suicide, offers suicide bereaved a comprehensive understanding of reasons and causes of the loss they grieve. Dr. Joiner's research into the serotonin transmitter gene suggests that this gene predisposes some people both to impulsivity and a proclivity to negative emotion. Dr. Joiner theorizes that death by suicide grows out of two psychological states. One is the perception of being a burden and the other is a feeling of not belonging. This theory, though somewhat painful, helps us understand that perception is the suicidal individual's viewpoint and not necessarily fact.

The books of Dr. Shneidman and Joiner are two of many good resources providing insight into the complexities of the suicidal state of mind. Read and learn, my friends. For learning and striving to understand strengthens us and enhances our healing.

About Grief

"There is sacredness in tears.
They are not the mark of weakness, but of power.
They speak more eloquently than ten thousand tongues.
They are the messenger of overwhelming grief,
of deep contrition, and unspeakable love."

Washington Irving

An understanding of grief and knowing what you are experiencing is normal may ease your journey.

Grief is what we feel inside, the emotions and thoughts that vary and vacillate within our mind and body after a beloved person dies. Acute grief experienced in the immediate aftermath of the death may manifest itself physically with nausea, body aches and headaches, chills, fever, and a sore throat. These are usually short-term. Grief after suicide involves emotional response to the cause of the death as well as to the fact of the death. When someone close deliberately ends their life, grief for the cause of death often temporarily supersedes grief for the fact of death.

Grief is not an ailment or a condition. It is the natural, necessary response to the death of someone in whom the survivor had a deep emotional investment. It is a psychic wound that takes time, care, and willingness to experience the pain in order to heal. You will not always hurt as badly as you do now. The obsessive, raging anguish suffered during acute grief eventually subsides into a more tolerable, more manageable mourning.

No two people experience grief in the same way. An individual's grief is as unique as a snowflake or a fingerprint. Grief differs depending upon the relationship with the person who died. There is a probability that your grief will be more painful than you would have thought possible. You may think you cannot endure it, but you can and you will.

Mourning, also known as grieving and grief work, is the outward expression of grief. As well as expressing and communicating grief, mourning is the process of adjusting emotional response, acknowledging the death as final, reconstructing one's life around the void created by the permanent absence, and reinvesting in a future where the deceased exists only in memory. Most important, mourning eventually involves reengaging in life—life forever changed.

Healthy mourning necessitates emotional, psychological, physical, social, and even spiritual adjustments to living without the person who died. In grief after suicide, healthy mourning necessitates adjustment to the cause of death, the shock, horror, inappropriateness, and stigma, as well as adjusting to the fact of death and the void death leaves behind.

Grief and mourning involve the entire person. As well as the emotional, psychological, social, and spiritual adjustments, the entire physical body is involved in acute grief and the mourning process. Not uncommonly, the digestive, muscular, skeletal, nervous, cardiovascular, lymphatic, and even the endocrine, urinary, and reproductive systems express the impact of grief. Chronic illness can worsen or illness in remission can become active. It is not unusual for menopausal-age women to experience early menses cessation or intensified menopausal symptoms. The newly bereaved may experience upset stomachs, aches and pains, heart palpitations, and sleep disorders. To protect your long-term mental and physical well-being after suffering acute bereavement, it is prudent to visit your physician within a few weeks of the bereavement to assure these symptoms are not indicative of illness.

Grief is not time limited or measurable. There is no time frame in which grief must or can be resolved and mourning completed. Every bereaved individual grieves at their own pace in their own space. Friends and extended family may expect or urge us to be over it in a few weeks or months. Although grief has no timetable, acute grief does not last forever, nor should it. There are suicide bereaved who seek the help of a grief counselor soon after the death. Some seek reinforcement and direction within a support group of suicide bereaved. Some do both. A few will needlessly try to suffer it out alone. After several months if you feel you haven't made progress in your mourning, it is prudent to seek the help of a grief counselor.

Grief work will take more energy than you would have imagined. Not uncommonly, bereaved feel exhausted, lethargic; just getting out of bed in the morning takes an almost concentrated effort. But grief can also produce energy, a feeling of restless disconnectedness where "grief energy" alternates with exhaustion and lethargy. Frenetic or hyper energy is uncomfortable because it has no place to go and nothing to do. This energy makes you say, "I feel as if I could jump out of my skin." Grief energy and the need to find a focus for it often propels bereaved persons toward positive activity and pursuits.

Grief is cyclic. Not uncommonly, a bereaved person expects to feel the sharpest, heaviest grief immediately following the loss. During the first hours or days following a death, the full burden of grief is anesthetized by shock and numbness. As the numbness wears off, the pain of grief may intensify. Sometimes within the first two or three months grief somewhat abates to return almost full force and recycles, not uncommonly in sixty to ninety day increments. This wave effect can cause bereaved persons concern about their emotional well-being. With each cycle the grief is expected to grow less acute, with longer spans of time between—expected, but this is not always the case. Holidays, birthdays, the death marker day, any special day shared with the person who has died will be especially tender and may trigger deep grief or anxiety for a time. Planning in advance how to spend that day can alleviate some of the anxiety of the occasion. Bereaved individuals often are filled with dread in the days leading up to a significant or tender day, then find that the actual day is not nearly as painful as they had feared it would be.

Men and women grieve differently. Women have their own nurturing system. They talk and talk and talk about every aspect of the death and their pain to a sympathetic "sister" who shares tears, tissues, and comforting hugs. Men often do not discuss their grief, some because they don't have the grief vocabulary to speak of their pain, some because they feel they don't have society's acceptance or permission to express their grief. Men admit they fear losing control: once they start crying they are afraid they won't be able to stop. Certainly men cry, and they should. There are men who will grieve openly and freely while others will shed their tears in private and work through their heartbreak in ways different from the ways women grieve. Men often focus their grief on busyness, tinkering with a car motor, repairing or building something, plowing the north forty, or going to the office, where surroundings are familiar and nonthreatening.

A support group participant shared concern that her husband wasn't grieving as he should because he didn't want to talk as she did at great length about their daughter's death and what happened, and he didn't cry openly or often. Women don't make the rules or set the pace for grieving. Most people grieve as they must, or as they have been modeled or conditioned. Males often have been conditioned to "suck it up" or told that "big boys don't cry." A suicide bereavement support group is a safe arena where men can give and accept permission to grieve and share what they have in common, overwhelming pain following the death of one dearly loved.

Disenfranchised grief is experienced when the loss cannot be openly acknowledged, socially sanctioned, or publicly mourned. When an unknown lover or same-sex partner dies, the bereaved family may exclude the surviving partner from the grieving circle, may deny or be unaware that the relationship exists. The bereaved lover or partner then mourns alone without acknowledgement of their loss and suffering. When the cause of death is suicide this mourner, if known, may be subjected to blame and censure by the immediate bereaved family. Grief does not discriminate. Any bereaved individual not permitted to grieve openly may find consolation and direction through counseling.

Complicated grief can be defined as acute grief that does not process and abate normally. Complicated grief, sometimes termed being "stuck," can last for months, even years, with the bereaved unable to move through grief to the normal diminishing of emotional pain and reconciliation with the loss. Complicated grief can be treated by a grief therapist.

Yardsticking grief is the need of some bereaved to quantify the pain of their loss. Our grief is our own, unique from any other. There is no benefit in trying to measure the loss or in thinking, "My loss is greater than yours; my pain is more." But growth and healing sometimes result from recognizing that the situation surrounding a loved one's death could have been even more traumatic and complicated.

There is no right or wrong way to grieve but there are healthy and unhealthy ways. Take the best possible care of yourself, your physical, mental, emotional, and spiritual body, in order for it to bear the weight of grief and allow you to live and prosper after your acute grief has subsided. Don't suppress, hide, or postpone your grief. Permit yourself to sob, to scream, to talk about what happened, to give your grief outlet and expression. Give your body respite by providing yourself an opportunity each day to be distracted from your grief, even momentarily. Lean into the pain and lean on those who offer to support you through it. On the other hand, beware of clinging to your grief or using it as a shield that prevents you from maintaining existing relationships or developing new ones. Consider attending a support group where you can interact with others who understand the meaning of loss through suicide.

Honor your grief. It has been said that grief is the price we pay for love, a price most people would pay even knowing that the cost of love would be the anguish of grief. You will grieve for what has been lost and for what you will never have. Honor your grief. Respect and embrace the pain of your loss and face it openly, freely, with dignity and integrity. Be patient with yourself in grief but be persistent in working through it.

You will experience remnants of grief for the death of your beloved throughout your life. Not unlike a treasured heirloom quilt, these fragments, remnants, irregular pieces represent joy you shared, sorrow for what you no longer have, and regret for what might have been. Each piece, whether colorful and glorious, faded or misshapen, tattered or a bit soiled is part of your life. Embrace your grief and the shared love it represents. Honor your grief by working through it, by coming to terms with your loss, by mastering it, by reinvesting in your future, where your heart will be warmed by loving memories.

Not All Loss Through Death Is the Same

"The risk of love is loss, and the price of loss is grief.
But the pain of grief is only a shadow
when compared with the pain of never risking love at all."

Hilary Stanton Zunin

The scope and intensity of loss experienced following a suicide is not one-size-fits-all. The breadth and depth of the loss depends upon the relationship, the survivor's circumstance, and cultural factors.

The nature and quality of the relationship with the deceased

Deb's only child, Mark, biracial and born out of wedlock when Deb was a nineteen-year-old college sophomore, caused temporary alienation from her socially prominent East Coast parents. After receiving her engineering degree, Deb accepted a position far from her family, remained unmarried, and devoted herself to raising Mark. She purchased a modest home; they skied, camped, hiked, and grew up together.

Mark, a bright, handsome, friendly boy, grew into a handsome, gregarious, gentle man, the sole focus and purpose of Deb's life. She was justifiably proud when Mark received his engineering degree with honors. Her pride was conflicted by apprehension when he accepted a substantial offer on the West Coast. His calls and letters vaguely hinted at discrimination, harassment, and disillusionment. They discussed ways they had coped with these issues during his youth. She visited him, saw his apartment, met his new friends, and was satisfied that in time everything would fall into place. Four months later Deb's world and her perceived reason for living were shattered by a call informing her that Mark had ended his life.

The survivors' emotional, social, physical, and, often, financial dependency upon the one who has died

High school sweethearts, Carla and Sid had been married thirty years when he ended his life. They had no children and considered themselves best friends, to the near total exclusion of others. Carla suffered a debilitating ailment that limited her mobility to a wheelchair, but she enjoyed telling how they danced, with Sid spinning and twirling her chair. Sid's suicide was devastating to Carla. His death deprived her of her closest friend and source of social interaction as well as her caretaker. Her grief involved addressing her perception that her disability had grown to be an unbearable burden to Sid and that he may have felt death was his only escape.

ℰ◌ℛ

At the time Amy's husband ended his life, they had two children, ages six months and eighteen months. Her grief was compounded by the loss of the family breadwinner, the loss of a parenting partner, and the need to comfort and care for her husband's mother, who had lost her only child. There were no savings and no life insurance. Until Social Security payment was forthcoming, there was no income. It was necessary for Amy to depend upon the generosity of friends and extended family to provide necessities for herself and her two babies. It was also necessary for her to find some means of supplementing Social Security during the most acute time of mourning.

Other sources of emotional investment and their availability

Tami was divorced when her only child, Chelsey, was a few months old. Chelsey's father was absent from their lives from that time on, making Tami Chelsey's sole parent and provider. They lived several hundred miles from extended family and spent many holidays and special occasions alone. Following Chelsey's sophomore year, after school was out in June, she received a letter advising her she had failed some courses that required repeating the coming school year. Tami immediately called the school. It was closed for the summer. Chelsey's enthusiasm for driving practice in preparation for her license came to a halt. She closed herself in her room and wouldn't talk to friends. Chelsey had no interest in their annual ritual of a weekend in a neighboring city to eat out, see a show, and shop for school clothes. In August, Chelsey ended her life. When the fall school session began, Tami went to the school and asked the principal why she hadn't been advised that Chelsey's grades required her to repeat classes. After the principal reviewed Chelsey's file, he told Tami Chelsey's grades were fine and the letter had been sent in error. He offered no apology, expressed no remorse, but did express concern whether Tami intended to bring suit against the school district. Weak with shock from learning that Chelsey's suicide was a response to someone's error, Tami was barely able to walk from the school building. Tami did not sue. She invested every ounce of her energy in her extreme struggle for survival.

Cultural and spiritual factors

Few other causes of death involve society's determination of God's judgment and condemnation. Both Christian and non-Christian religions have condemned suicide; most cultures do as well. In a little mountain town the funeral for Dan and Debra's seventeen-year-old daughter was delayed several days while the foreign-born clergyman consulted superiors for assurance that performing burial rites for a suicide would not jeopardize his position in the church. The delay negatively impacted church members and placed Dan and Debra outside the comfort circle of their faith-based community, depriving them of a critical source of solace at the time they needed it most.

Law enforcement responders after Dale's wife ended her life confiscated her computer, several scratch pads, and the contents of an ashtray that was close to her body. Overhearing a comment about the investigation, Dale believed these effects were taken because suicide was a crime. Because his belief was based on action by someone in a position of authority, a policeman, Dale was convinced his wife had committed a crime by ending her life. This belief complicated his grief with a deep sense of shame. *A violent death scene is treated as a crime scene until the cause of death has been determined.*

Recent and concurrent losses

When losses occur in rapid succession, the survivor has little time to cope with one loss before the next occurs. There seems little about one loss or grief experience that prepares the bereaved for another loss, then another or yet another.

Mary, the youngest of five sisters, had her first experience with death at age ten when her twenty-three-year-old brother-in-law died of cancer. Mary learned the harsh reality that death was permanent and irreversible. She grieved the loss of her "brother," but most of all, she grieved for her pregnant sister and three-year-old niece who had lost their husband and father.

Mary was in her mid-twenties, married with two children, when her father was killed in an automobile accident. Her reaction to his unexpected death was shock and deep sorrow. Suddenly, her lifetime hero was gone. Mary found solace in knowing that, at age seventy-five, her father had lived a full life and had left her wonderful memories. Her immediate grief was diverted to concern for her mother and sister who were severely injured in the same accident.

Nine years later Mary's mother died of natural causes at age eighty-three. After her mother's death, Mary's deepest sense of loss was the loss of the family home—not just the physical structure but where the family had always gathered and where the heart went to be renewed. The sisters pledged to meet at least once a year and stay connected so that, even without a physical home, they would remain a close family.

In the spring of 1992, a beloved nephew died of AIDS. Mary felt great sorrow for his loss but was deeply troubled by the family's lack of integrity in their mourning. Every family member grieved but each deliberately avoided mentioning the cause of his death. Mary found it difficult to comfort her sister who, although heartbroken, was ashamed of why he died.

On November 9, 1992, Mary found seventeen-year-old Jeremy, her only son, dead of a self-inflicted gunshot. This was Mary's greatest loss, her deepest wound. She was inconsolable and questioned whether she could go on living. No words could describe the devastating impact upon Mary's family. What was he thinking? There was no explanation of why he would do such a thing. The decision was made to be truthful about the cause of Jeremy's death, to hold their heads high and not to give credence to stigma. Mary carried a tremendous burden of guilt for not having known Jeremy was suffering such despair, believing she should have known and been able to help him. Her husband's strength and the need to love and guide her two surviving daughters helped Mary survive Jeremy's death.

Four years later Mary's nephew was found dead from an apparent drug overdose. In addition to the shock and pain of losing another family member, Mary witnessed the horrendous treatment of her sister and her nephew's family by authorities. The police showed total disregard for the family's feelings and apparently assumed, since her nephew had long hair, arms full of tattoos, and used drugs, that he had no value and the family deserved no consideration or compassion. His grief-stricken mother's response to the crude indifference directed toward her and her dead son: "No matter how he looked he was somebody. He was someone's son and someone's daddy and he deserved respect." This was yet another experience with the cruelty a socially unacceptable death can cause people to display.

Mary's most recent experience with death was the murder of her sister during a home burglary. The crime occurred in an average family home in a quiet neighborhood in Baltimore. Her sister was violated and savagely beaten to death. The criminal was arrested and brought to trial. During the trial Mary heard every explicit detail of the crime and how her sister suffered. The emotional pain was almost more than Mary could bear, as if she was personally experiencing her sister's torture. Mary's only consolation was that the perpetrator was caught, tried, convicted, and sentenced to life in prison.

Mary is a tiny woman with a gigantic heart who has courageously channeled her numerous grief and mourning experiences into action that helps others who have suffered loss, especially through suicide. Mary and her husband have been involved in HEARTBEAT, a suicide bereavement support group, since soon after their son's death, first as newly bereaved and later as leaders. After being trained, Mary presented suicide prevention education to high school students, a high-risk population, teaching them to recognize and appropriately respond to suicide risk among their peers. Mary is survivor epitomized.

The circumstance and cause of the loss

The cause of the loss, the manner of the death, not uncommonly makes a difference in the emotional impact as well as in the reaction of one's social community.

Carol Graham displays a picture of her three college-age children standing on the Great Wall of China during a family vacation and recalls, "I felt like the luckiest mother in the world to have such amazing children. At that moment our world was perfect."

June 21, 2003, then-Colonel Mark Graham and his wife, Carol, stationed in Korea, received word that their youngest son, twenty-one-year-old Kevin, had hanged himself from his bedroom ceiling fan in the apartment he shared with his brother, Jeffrey, and his sister, Melanie. The siblings were students at the University of Kentucky. Melanie found Kevin when she went to his room to learn why he hadn't kept an early morning golf date with his brother.

A bright, handsome, soft-spoken pre-med student and ROTC cadet, Kevin was diagnosed with depression in October 2002 after participating in a university depression screening. He was seen at the university clinic by a mental health professional, who prescribed an antidepressant. Without consulting a doctor Kevin discontinued taking his antidepressant in the weeks before his death. Kevin's grades slipped, threatening his life-long dream of being an army doctor. His father shares that Kevin was a perfectionist who never felt anything he did was good enough. Mark wonders if they pushed their son too hard. Kevin's family believes the rigorous pre-med workload and pressure deeply affected Kevin; he feared losing his ROTC scholarship if it became known he was on a psychiatric medication. Mark told Kevin not to worry about the scholarship and offered to pay back the scholarship funds, but Kevin said, "No, I don't want to be a quitter." Major General Graham's last words to his son were, "I love you, son." General Graham reflects, "I knew my son was sad, but what I didn't know was that you could die from being too sad."General Graham's words echo the remorse of many suicide-bereaved parents: "I will blame myself for the rest of my life that I didn't do more to help my son."

Carol Graham, with a master's degree in counseling, suffers terribly from not having recognized the depth and deadliness of Kevin's depression. During one overseas telephone call Kevin asked his mother, "Did you know that depression is an illness, not just a feeling?" In another telephone conversation Kevin told her, "Mom, I don't think my brain works anymore."She doesn't recall what she answered but believes that Kevin was trying to tell her how troubled he was. She says, "I know now that I should have gotten on the first plane from Korea to Kentucky and hired the best psychiatrist I could find."

"After Kevin died we felt like the absolute worst parents in the world, like failures, like we hadn't loved our son enough." Carol said. Although Carol and Mark knew some relatives had been hospitalized due to mental illness, neither of them thought of depression as a mental illness. They had never discussed it and, certainly, never talked with their children about it. After Kevin's death several family members shared with Mark and Carol that they were taking medication for depression but had kept it private. Carol strongly believes it is important that family members be made aware when depression is diagnosed and is being treated within the family. *Although suicide is not inherited, genetics can play a part in mental illness.*

The Grahams' oldest son, Jeffrey, graduated from college just prior to his brother's death and was commissioned an army lieutenant. Mark and Carol describe Jeffrey as "always the cool one," an athlete, always with a smile on his face, and an attitude that the glass was always more than half full. The army offered Jeffrey the option of staying stateside to train other soldiers. He refused the offer of a non-combat-unit position, saying he needed to be with his platoon. He told his fiancée that the only thing worse than being at war was being a soldier and not being at war. Jeffrey deployed to Iraq in November 2003.

February 19, 2004, seven months after Kevin's death, Second Lt. Jeffrey Graham died in Kalidiyah, Iraq, near Fallujah, when an improvised explosive device exploded, killing him and another soldier. Carol said, "When I learned Jeffrey was dead I knew that Kevin was right there when that bomb exploded and he caught him and they were together again."

Jeffrey Graham was the first Kentucky soldier to die in Iraq. He was buried with full military honors. After Jeffrey's death the Grahams expressed their awareness of how differently the two deaths had been addressed both by the military and by friends. Parents of children killed in combat receive a gold star and are often invited as a group to meet with the president or other dignitaries. They receive a letter from the president of the United States expressing sympathy and acknowledging the sacrifice that was made in preservation of our country's freedom. After Jeffrey died the Grahams were told repeatedly how heroic their son was.

There was no such recognition for Kevin. After Kevin's self-inflicted death the Grahams debated whether to have his burial be private to protect the family. Mark and Carol Graham are forever grateful for being supported in their choice to bury Kevin as if his death had been by any other cause.

The deaths of both their boys caused the Grahams indescribable pain, but Kevin's was especially troubling because it was unexpected and self-inflicted. Carol invested her grief energy in speaking about depression and suicide at conferences and workshops. Her message that depression must be recognized as a medical illness is loud and clear. Carol found solace in sharing her story and being with other suicide bereaved. She accepted an invitation to serve on the board of Suicide Prevention Action Network, a national suicide prevention agency. Carol expresses her hope, "Maybe other people's kids will be saved by hearing our story."

Mark's initial response was quite different. Outwardly he showed little emotion. He chose not to speak about Kevin's death and adopted a business-as-usual demeanor, a response not unfamiliar in the military, whose members remain very uncomfortable discussing suicide. After Jeffrey died Mark agreed to speak at a TAPS (Tragedy Assistance Program for Survivors) conference in Washington D.C. Knowing TAPS as a program for survivors of military-related deaths, Mark fully expected to speak about Jeffrey's death in Iraq. But Bonnie Carroll, founder and director of TAPS, wanted him to talk about depression and the circumstance of Kevin's suicide.

Since his TAPS presentation General Mark Graham has combined the passion of his grief and his bitterly gained knowledge with the power of his position as a base commander to change the way the military responds to depression and suicide. Kevin's father has not deviated from his mission to reduce the stigma of getting mental health help in the military. He is works unceasingly to assure that military personnel can and will seek the help that is available, free from fear of reprisal.

"Both my sons were warriors" stated General Graham at a conference in Denver. "Both my boys died battling an enemy and to their mother and me, they are both heroes." He continues, "Our story is one of unbelievable sorrow but we know that sorrow endured in the right spirit increases our growth." And thus, General Mark Graham's battle for the freedom of other soldiers to access life-preserving services spreads from base to base to Washington, D.C., and beyond.

Melanie Graham, Mark and Carol's surviving child, sought counseling to work through the trauma of finding her brother, Kevin and to reconcile with the deaths of both Kevin and Jeffrey and the change of her identity from the sister of two brothers to an only child. Since their deaths Melanie completed her nurse's training and works as a neurology nurse at Beth Israel Hospital in Boston. Following the example of her parents, Melanie shared her version of the Grahams' story with Jeanne Blake of "Words Can Work" in a handbook on depression entitled *Words Can Work When Talking About Depression*. Carol believes sharing her perspective on the tragedies of her brother's death was a turning point for her daughter. In 2010, in a glorious summer wedding, Melanie married Joseph Quinn, a young military man with whom she shares in common the tragedy of a brother's death. James Quinn, Joseph's brother, died on the 101st floor of the World Trade Center North Tower, September 11, 2001.

Not All Grief Is the Same

*"I measure every grief I meet with analytic eyes,
I wonder if it weighs like mine, or has an easier size."*

Emily Dickinson

My personal grief experiences allow me to verify this chapter's title.

The middle child of our five children, our only daughter, Karen, died in May 2006 of an illness. At the time of her death Karen was forty-nine years old. Married twenty-seven years, she had two grown children and a grandson. My emotional reaction to her death caused me to better understand that each loss, each grief experience is as unique as the relationship shared with that person. The scope of my grief for the deaths of each of my beloved children is beyond measure or description. But my grief reactions can be defined to some extent. Emotional reactions to my son's sudden, self-inflicted death included shock, horror, disbelief, and trauma; then guilt, anger, embarrassment, despair, and a tremendous sense of failure as a parent.

Kent had moved back into our home to attend a local college. After his death we were faced with the void created by his absence in our household as well as the task of sorting through and disposing of his personal belongings. We were also faced with the room in our home where he had inflicted the fatal injury and the incomprehensible fact that he had deliberately caused his own death and we had been unaware of the pain he was suffering. Additionally, there was the stigma that accompanies death by suicide.

My grief following my daughter's death was certainly not less, nor greater, but different, more subdued and controlled. I had been deeply shocked when I learned the extent of her illness and disbelieving when I was told it would very likely shorten her life. Her healthy appearance and attitude offered me the shelter of denial. I chose to believe she would outlive me.

The closeness we had shared as she was growing up had matured into deep adult friendship. There had been time for the two of us to acknowledge together the prospect of her shortened life. She asked how I thought she would be remembered and she talked of how she wanted "things" to be. She voiced her concern for her children's well-being and her grandson's future and asked that I "look after" her family. We often reminisced about the past and her love of fun, jokes, and mischief. We were able to speak of, even laugh about, friction during her teen years and forgive one another for slights, hurts, and misunderstandings.

Experiential and intellectual understanding of grief allowed me to know the suffocating pain I was experiencing was normal, even though that knowledge didn't make it easier to bear. Knowing that her time might be limited allowed me to hold her, share with her, to tell her what a beautiful person she was and how proud I was of her. Knowing gave me a chance to brace myself for death's approach and for a future I could not imagine, a future without her. Her death caused me no guilt, no anger at her, no embarrassment . . . but profound, soul-searing sorrow.

After the suicide of my son I had a persistent need to separate and define my complex and overwhelming emotional reactions. What I learned over time about compounded grief assures me that what I was experiencing was normal for what I had gone through. Social, philosophical, and religious influences intensify, magnify, and complicate emotional response to death. As we review these factors our understanding of the complexity of suicide grief grows.

The age of the deceased

Many who deliberately end their lives are young, some as young as eight or nine years of age. A large proportion of suicides cut their life expectancy in half or more, leaving a legacy of unfulfilled dreams complicated by an intense sense of guilt. The sense of guilt or unmet responsibility is usually greater among parents of young suicides. As one's child grows toward adulthood, parental authority is relinquished and parents are able to view their children as using their own judgment, responsible for themselves, and accountable for their own actions. The parent of an older child recognizes there were beyond-the-family environmental influences involved in the child's action over which the parent had no control.

Whether the death was sudden or anticipated

Suicide is perceived as a sudden death. Even when indicators of risk have been recognized, the probability that the individual would actually end their life may be denied. This places a magnified sense of neglect and responsibility upon the survivor aware of risk but unable to prevent or respond. The preparations made and the emotional processing in some incidents of anticipatory grief do not apply when the death results from suicide.

Whether the death was peaceful or violent

Suicide is a violent death regardless of the means used to cause the death. Quite often the method of death leaves the survivor with ghastly and indelible images of the mutilation the deceased inflicted upon themselves. Even in incidents where the body is not mutilated, the death is violence against the self.

Whether the death was random or intentional

Suicide is intentional. Although the intent to die may be debatable, the fact that the fatal injury was deliberately self-inflicted raises the usually unanswerable question, *Why?* The implied intent assaults every aspect of the survivor's being by raising the question of the survivor's role in the decedent's despair. The implied intent lays bare, for society's judgment and censure, the survivor's ability to adequately perform their role in their relationship with the deceased. That the act was intentionally self-inflicted implies rejection, abandonment, and broken trust.

Whether the death was preventable

At some point, many suicides are preventable. It is obvious that the 35,000 suicides occurring each year in our nation were not prevented, but how many may have been preventable? The survivor aware of the decedent's suicide risk may experience a heavy burden of unmet responsibility for not having been constantly available as guardian. More often than not, suicide bereaved had no foreknowledge or training that enabled them to recognize the imminentness of suicide. Yet, almost without exception, survivors see themselves as the rescuer who failed, that somehow they should have known and prevented what took place. Or they believe that had they known and been available, they would have prevented it. It is not unusual for someone bereaved by suicide to develop an immediate sense of their own omnipotence: "If I had only known I could have kept it from happening"; "If I had been there she would still be alive."

Whether the cause of death was appropriate or inappropriate

Suicide is the most socially, philosophically, and religiously inappropriate of all causes of death. In most of the world it is

not socially, philosophically or religiously acceptable to deliberately end one's own life or to have a family member do so.
By ending his/her own life, the deceased has crossed a taboo
boundary. The survivors must cope with their own biases and
beliefs about suicide based in teachings from earlier years
regarding those who deliberately end their lives. Not uncommonly, they feel the lashings of stigma and suffer judgment and
condemnation from their social and religious communities.

Not All Grief After Suicide Is the Same

*"Take this sorrow unto thy heart, and make it part of thee,
and it shall nourish thee til thou art strong again."*

Henry Wadsworth Longfellow, *Hyperion*

There are situations when the compounding issues surrounding death by suicide are magnified by the circumstance of the death. Sharing complex suicide scenarios can point to the indomitable strength of the human spirit and show how people can live through and beyond more than they ever would believe possible. It can be important, even strengthening, for bereaved readers to recognize that, while their loss is the worst thing that has ever happened to them, there are suicide bereaved who endure an unbelievable level of horror yet somehow cope, reconcile, and build a bountiful life beyond their tragedy. When we learn of survivors who have undergone extremely complicated suicide loss situations we ask ourselves, "How did they endure the pain and live through and beyond the horror of their tragedies?"

A college sophomore, twenty-one year old Susan, the oldest of Jean and Bob's two children, was hospitalized following her second suicide attempt in four months. She was diagnosed with bipolar illness, and treated with medication and therapy. Upon her release from the hospital her doctors warned Jean and Bob that Susan's mental health was fragile. They took her home where they believed she would be safer. When Susan ended her life a few months later Bob and Jean's grief was beyond intense but they had great sympathy for Susan and some understanding of her torment and struggle. They were comforted knowing that everything that could have been done for Susan, had been done.

Two years after Susan's death, when their surviving child, nineteen year old Scott, deliberately shot and killed himself their emotional response was very different. Their shock and horror and despair was compounded by intense anger at Scott. Although Scott and Susan had never been close and he had not seemed deeply affected by her death, he was very aware of the impact of Susan's illness and death upon them. He had been loving and comforting. Jean and Bob shared some of their emotional reactions following Scott's death: As their only living child he knew they needed and depended upon him. He was strong and healthy, with years to live and he gave them up, for what and why? They were angry, frustrated, and deeply sorrowful for the senselessness of Scott's death and the waste of his life. They felt betrayed and rejected by Scott as they struggled to understand why he would end his life knowing how much it would hurt them.

Jean and Bob were lovingly comforted and reinforced by friends and members of both their work communities. Their bond with one another, therapy and a support group helped them cope during the early months of their mourning. A few months following Scott's death, with mixed feelings, they looked toward a new beginning after Bob's company transferred him to another state.

෨෬

Lisa described the four of them as a perfect Norman Rockwell family: good jobs as teachers, with her husband, Louis, a candidate for an administrative position, supportive families, two healthy daughters, a modest but comfortable lifestyle, and very much in love.

On February 9, 2009, as Louis drove her to school, they talked of plans with their daughters, Mari and JL, for the following weekend, Valentine's Day. Louis pulled up in front of Lisa's school and leaned over to kiss her before driving on to his school. Lisa grinned at the catcalling students and went into school thinking "Life is good."

At 11:30, Lisa's cell phone rang in her classroom. She didn't recognize the number and didn't answer. She ignored a second ring. She then received a call from the school office telling her to answer her phone immediately. The call was from a Detective Meade who, after confirming Lisa's identity, told Lisa her daughters were safely in custody at Safe Passages, a protective agency for abused children, and ordered her to come immediately. The detective directed Lisa, "Do not call your husband!" School staff quickly responded to Lisa's emergency, someone taking her class and another driving her to Safe Passages.

Her heart pounding, Lisa walked into Safe Passages and a semicircle of law enforcement personnel, representatives from both her and her husband's school districts, and Department of Social Services staff. After Lisa was assured her daughters were there and safe, she turned to the detective for an explanation. Lisa was informed that the oldest daughter, fourteen-year-old Mari, had told her counselor that her father was sexually molesting her and that she was afraid for her younger sister. The school reported it to the authorities who picked up the girls and held them at Safe Passage. Horrified, Lisa asked to talk with Mari, concerned that she might have told her counselor an untruth because she was angry at her dad for grounding her cell phone. After Lisa was convinced Mari was telling the truth, she asked Mari why she hadn't told her this was happening. Mari replied that daddy said this was their secret and if she told mommy or Nona (his mother) they would be very, very upset with her. Mari was examined and her claim authenticated. Lisa's immediate concern was custody of her daughters. After lengthy questioning, the authorities were convinced Lisa had no knowledge of the abuse and she was assured her children would remain in her custody. A court order was issued prohibiting Louis from being with them.

Lisa received a call from Louis on her cell phone telling her he had just been put on administrative leave and did she know what the @%# was going on. She said, "Louis, Mari told your secret. She says you abused her. Is that true?" Louis hung up.

Law enforcement asked Lisa if Louis had a gun in his posses-
sion, and she assured them he did not. She gave them permission
to search the family's house and computers. Louis called again
and said that police were at their house. Lisa told him she'd
given permission for the search and asked again if he had hurt
their daughter. Louis didn't answer her question but said, "You
know I will never get an administrative position now." Lisa said,
"Yes, I know." Louis terminated the call. The police asked Lisa
if she would make a call to Louis that could be recorded for
use in court. She agreed. She called Louis. He did not answer.
After several unanswered calls she left him a message telling
him she needed to know where he was and where the car was,
and adding that if he did not answer she was going to call his
mother. When Louis finally answered, Lisa asked where he was.
Louis told her, "The car is in the Sears parking lot. I love you and
the girls. I will see you in the afterlife." Lisa screamed at him,
"Louis, don't you dare do that to the girls! You know what it did
to me when my dad killed himself!" After the call ended Lisa
remembered they had gone shooting several weeks before and
that the gun might still be in the trunk of the car. An APB was
put out to find Louis. A few minutes later, as Detective Meade
walked toward Lisa, the look on the detective's face confirmed
Lisa's fear: Louis had shot himself and was being transported
to the hospital.

The social worker would not allow Lisa to take her daughters to the hospital. Lisa called Louis's parents to tell them
Louis had shot himself, that he was in the hospital and they
should come. When Lisa arrived at the hospital, she learned
Louis would not live, but because he was an organ donor he
was being kept on life support until Lisa could sign the papers
for donation. She signed the donor papers and left the hospital.
She needed to be with her girls and did not want to be at the
hospital when Louis's family arrived. Lisa had always had a loving relationship with them, but they were a large, emotionally
demonstrative family dominated by Louis's mother. Lisa knew
she would lose control if she had to see their pain or offer any

explanations to them at that time. Maintaining control was the fragile bridge between sanity and a complete breakdown.

Lisa told her daughters their father was dead. Mari's immediate response was, "It's my fault. I should never have told." Lisa firmly held Mari's chin as she told her, "Mari, this was not your fault. Don't ever think it was your fault. You did what you should have done. Daddy felt terrible shame for what he did. That's why he died. But that's daddy's shame . . . it's not yours, and not mine." As an indescribably harsh and painful day came to a close, Lisa was finally allowed to take her daughters home.

Louis's family called. They objected to organ donation. They did not want Louis's body cremated. They wanted to talk to Mari. Louis's brother wanted to do the eulogy. A funeral for Louis was not important to Lisa, but she knew his family and her girls needed to have one. She planned services for Louis at the church where his family were members, using the funeral home the family had always relied upon.

Just after midnight on Tuesday Lisa received a call from the Donor Alliance representative. The organ harvest had been completed. Louis was officially dead.

Lisa began assessing her financial situation. Their bank account was frozen. She had no money, no car, and no husband. She was very angry at Louis. She cried and cried and screamed at him that if he hadn't killed himself she would have done it for him. Louis was vested in the educational retirement program, so the girls were eligible for those funds and Social Security. The life insurance policy Louis had with the district had been in force only eighteen months and did not meet the exclusion requirement of two years. Premiums paid would be returned. With the help of her mother, stepfather, and friends she got the car out of impound, retrieved $200 that had been in Louis's billfold, and tried to plan for what came next.

On Wednesday Lisa and her daughters had the first of many weekly therapy sessions. Lisa's once-loving relationship with

Louis's family deteriorated until there was little or no inter-action. Although Lisa encouraged visits from them she was adamant that the visits be supervised to avoid Mari being ques-tioned and guilt heaped upon her. The family rejected further opportunity to interact with Louis's daughters, causing Mari and JL to also lose their large extended family.

More than two years since Louis's death, Lisa and her daugh-ters are still adapting, Lisa to the responsibilities of being the sole parent, Mari to her senior year and planning for college, and JL to life as a busy middle-school student. Counseling has been put on hold for the present. Mari seems to have fewer trust issues around males than her mother, who struggles to keep her composure whenever a male directs attention toward Mari. Lisa understands why Louis ended his life and has for-given him for leaving her and their daughters, but she doubts that she will ever find forgiveness for his molestation of Mari and his betrayal of their once-perfect family.

℘℘

Laura shares her family's tragedy with hope it will give an-other survivor encouragement. Laura's only son, Sammy, grew up with an abusive, alcoholic, but financially successful father. Sammy began using drugs in his early twenties and continued to use off and on throughout his life. Despite unsuccessful ef-forts at rehabilitation, Sammy was always an attentive son to his mother and supportive to his sisters, Cassie and Janet. He adored his wife, Twila, their four-year-old son, Markie, and Mona, his eight-year-old daughter from a previous marriage.

After Sammy began using steroids to "buff up," his personali-ty changed drastically. His behavior was erratic, and he became enraged over little things. His concerned family pleaded with him to get help. Sammy rejected their pleas, denying he had a problem.

The evening of December 19, 2002, Sammy met his two nephews to celebrate winning custody of Mona after months of court battles with his ex-wife. In the early hours of December 20, 2002, a 911 call from Mona told the operator her daddy had been drinking and had a gun. She was afraid he was going to hurt Twila. The call abruptly ended after a voice shouted, "Mona, who did you call?" Police immediately responded to find that Sammy had shot and killed Twila, Markie, and Mona before killing himself.

Cassie heard an early morning news report of shooting deaths at her brother's address. She called Janet and their mother and they immediately went to the scene. They found the street near Sammy's house roped off and lined with police, emergency, and coroner vehicles. The apartment entrance was obscured by sheets that had been draped to prevent bystanders from viewing the investigation and removal of the bodies.

Laura's grief for her son was compounded to an overwhelming degree by the additional losses of Twila, with whom she'd shared deep affection, and her beloved grandchildren, Markie and Mona. Laura has little recall of the weeks following this tragedy when she was so deeply wounded, defeated, and isolated. She has no wish to remember. She was angry at God for allowing this tragedy to happen and extremely angry at Sammy for causing it. For several months following the deaths, Laura was convinced that somehow she was responsible for Sammy's action. In the early spring she suffered an emotional collapse and was hospitalized and treated for severe depression.

Laura had always thrived on work, but she could not resume the activity level she had formerly enjoyed. Through trial and error, she learned what was and was not good for her. Volunteering became Laura's lifeline. Early in her grief she volunteered at a local anti-domestic-violence organization, doing clerical work and making blankets for the many babies housed there. She visited nursing homes and did small kindnesses for residents who seldom had visitors. Laura volunteered because she loved helping people and needed to be useful; helping others helped her. Laura knows that doing something to lift the spirits of others lifts her up and makes her feel better about herself. Feeling better about herself is an ongoing struggle for Laura.

Following months of therapy Laura felt strong enough to volunteer as a speaker to young drug offenders in the county diversion program. During her presentations she showed pictures of Sammy and his family during their good times. She told of Sammy's drug addiction and the tragic consequence of his drug use. Her powerful story made a strong impact on the young offenders, bringing tears and causing many of them to write her notes of appreciation, declaring their decision never to use drugs again. The emotional toll of reliving the tragedy during these presentations caused Laura's involvement in this program to be short lived but she has been rewarded by knowing that sharing her story, even a few times, made a difference.

Laura believes progress in her healing was initially compromised by a stressful job, stressful people, and memories of stressful events. Her daughter, Cassie, moved Laura into her home in a neighboring city so she could monitor her mother's well-being. As Laura improved she moved into a cozy apartment in a retirement complex, eventually working a few hours a week in a department store.

The tragedy reduced Laura's family to seven members. Bit by bit they have learned what restores them and how they can best survive. Laura and her daughters enjoy time in their kitchens chatting and laughing as they prepare favorite foods for the family that gathers frequently to share meals and exchange loving reinforcement. By unspoken agreement, no heated arguments, harsh words, or discussions of unpleasant events occur during their gatherings. The entire family focuses on expressing love and support of one another. In the years since the deaths this practice has helped Laura's family grow stronger and closer as they reaffirm that love and kindness is every bit as contagious and much more powerful than criticism and anger.

Laura continues to have moments of deep despair and knows it is likely she always will. She has learned to protect her fragile emotional health by depending upon the strength of her faith and the joy and security of loving relationships with her surviving family. She relies upon her therapists when she feels the need and enjoys the distraction of meeting the public a few hours a week in her work. An attractive, intelligent woman, Laura greets fellow residents in her retirement building with a cheerfulness that belies the heartache she suffers. She is firm in her belief that she survives this tragedy because her work on earth is not yet done.

As Laura speaks of her son and her surviving family, she sadly muses, "Sammy left a family of shattered souls. We all are doing our best to move ahead. I don't know why Sammy did this terrible thing. What he did was not my son. I now know I am not responsible for Sammy's act. Sammy is responsible. Sammy had many choices and he made some very bad ones. I must live with and beyond his bad choices by doing what I know is best for me."

℘℘℘

While there is no way to measure grief, some bereaved endure loss and grief beyond the most horrendous nightmares. Sue and her family have endured the ultimate horror and pain, and they embody courage and resiliency. As a guest speaker at a suicide bereavement conference Sue shared a PowerPoint presentation beginning with a picture of herself with her son, Dylan, at his fifth birthday celebration, a tousle-headed Dylan on a tricycle, a young teen Dylan wearing a baseball cap and finally, Dylan dressed in a tuxedo for his senior prom date. On April 20, 1999, three days after the prom picture was taken, Dylan Klebold, 17, and Eric Harris, 18, murdered twelve fellow students and a teacher and wounded twenty-four others in a shooting spree at their school, Columbine High School in Littleton, Colo. The shootings lasted about forty minutes and ended when Dylan and Eric shot and killed themselves.

As Sue was dressing for work that morning she called out to Dylan when she heard him leaving for school and received a brusque "bye" in response. This was to be the last time Sue heard Dylan's voice. Around noon at her workplace Sue listened to a frightening message left by her husband telling her to call him immediately, there was an emergency. Her first thought was that one of her sons had been in an accident. When she returned his call her husband told her he had received a call from one of Dylan's friends telling of a shooting at the high school and that it was believed people in black trench coats were the gunmen. Dylan often wore a black trench coat. The friend knew the students who wore trench coats and said all were accounted for except Dylan and his friend Eric. Sue feared Dylan was among those shot. She was frantic in her concern for his safety as she drove home.

At home Sue's husband told her he had been unable to find Dylan's trench coat and feared that Dylan was involved in the shooting. A SWAT team arrived and informed Sue, her husband, and their twenty-year-old son that they must leave the house so a search could be conducted. For the rest of the afternoon the three of them sat on the sidewalk or paced back and forth waiting for news. Through open windows they could hear on-scene news coverage of the carnage. Late in the afternoon they were informed that Dylan was dead. Then it was confirmed that Dylan and Eric were the perpetrators in the massacre at Columbine and after killing thirteen and wounding twenty-four people, they had shot and killed themselves. News helicopters hovered overhead and cars drove slowly by their home seeking a glimpse or photo of a Columbine shooter's family.

The parents of Dylan and Eric were vilified around the world. According to one newspaper survey, 85 percent of respondents believed the boys' parents were at fault for the tragedy. Sue coped by numbing herself to the outside world. She didn't read the newspaper or listen to the local news reports of the shootings. She stopped watching television because viewing the anguish of the victim's friends and family's made her nearly insane with sorrow. Her horror was compounded when it was learned from Dylan and Eric's journals that had their plans not gone awry, they would have blown up the entire school.

Hate mail began arriving, most blaming them for the shootings and referring to Dylan as a monster. It was impossible for Sue to view Dylan, the son she had so lovingly raised, as a monster even though she acknowledged that his monstrous acts caused terrible suffering. Both the Klebold and Harris parents sent messages to the grieving families expressing their deep sorrow for the deaths their sons had caused.

Thirty-six lawsuits were filed against Dylan's family. They could not attend a grief group for suicide bereaved due to the pending lawsuits. Sue was able to begin therapy only after their attorney located a therapist who was not engaged by or acquainted with any of the victim's families. Their family and close friends stood by them. Sue was eventually allowed to join a suicide survivor support group where she could relate, to some extent, with other parents who had lost children to suicide. Sue counts as a special blessing an invitation to meet with a few of the victim's families who extended compassion to her.

Dylan's parents are a highly intelligent and well-educated couple described by neighbors as gentle, caring people. A former neighbor said, "They raised their boys like we all do." Tom Klebold operated a mortgage management business from his home. Sue Klebold helped train disabled students for the work world in the Colorado community college system. In March the family had made a trip with Dylan to visit the University of Arizona, where he had been accepted. His father reportedly said, "I thought we had a fine, finished product." Sue defended their parenting by saying, "Dylan did not commit this crime because of how he was raised but in complete contradiction to how he was raised."

Dylan and Eric were intelligent young men from solid two-parent homes who met and became friends in middle school. Later they worked at the same pizza parlor and spent time together playing computer games. In January 1998, they were arrested for breaking into a van and spent several months in a juvenile diversion program attending workshops, talking with counselors, and working on a volunteer project. They appeared to be repentant. For months after the program's conclusion, Dylan and Eric saw little of one another. Then gradually they began spending time together again. Eric even slept over one weekend night before the shootings. Their journals revealed that Dylan and Eric were planning the Columbine killings during the time they were in the juvenile diversion program. Any hope that Dylan had been an accidental participant or had been coerced into participating evaporated.

Every year on April 20, and every time there is a student shooting or the threat of one, the media reminds the world of the Columbine tragedy. Sue and her family need no reminder. They still encounter hateful comments. They still struggle with the horror of what Dylan was responsible for as they try to establish a tolerable level of normalcy in their lives. Sue has undergone hundreds of hours of therapy. She has delved deeply into the study of suicide in an effort to understand Dylan's state of mind. She honors the loving memory of a darling five-year-old Dylan, a kid in a baseball cap, and a near-grown Dylan on his way to the prom, by advocating suicide prevention awareness for all people. She specifically encourages parents of youth to prepare themselves to recognize and appropriately respond to symptoms of depression.

Sue ended her conference PowerPoint presentation with, "I will never be able to explain, excuse or atone for what Dylan did, but I hope by hearing my story those who can still be helped, will be helped."

Jean and Bob, Lisa, Laura, Sue, and other courageous people who share how they survived their tragedies do so believing that there may be others in similar circumstances who will find comfort, strength, and hope from knowing that someone else has endured, grown strong, and once again found satisfaction in life.

Suicide Grief Strata

*"Grief is a wound that needs attention in order to heal.
To work through and complete grief
means to face our feelings openly and honestly,
to express or release our feelings fully,
and to tolerate and accept our feelings for however
long it takes for the wound to heal."*

Judy Tatelbaum, *The Courage to Grieve*

Grief is a normal response to the death of someone deeply loved. It is often described as coming in phases, stages, levels, waves, or layers. Grief following suicide is extremely chaotic, complex, compounded and fiercely painful. Be aware that varying levels or intensity of grief will not come in sequence and not all responses in all strata will be experienced by all bereaved. There will be some overlap and repetition as you work through the pain of your loss toward a time when the raging anguish subsides and a gentler, more manageable state of mourning evolves.

For suicide bereaved to know "what I am experiencing is normal for what I have experienced" is reassuring. The following outline of suicide grief strata is intended to inform and reassure.

RECOIL—The knee-buckling gut punch upon learning of a significant other's suicide

Shock, horror, numbness, disbelief, confusion, denial (often a primary defense)

Compounded trauma = fact of death + cause of the death (cause of death is commonly the primary trauma)

Search for answers—need to know why—begins immediately

Physical manifestations—flu like symptoms = body aches, chills, sore throat, upset stomach, diarrhea (short-term) heart palpitations, breathing difficulty, concentration problems memory lapse, sleep problems (longer term)

REACTION—Chaotic Emotional Response

Disorientation and discord—rejection/denial of the fact of suicide

Anger, fear, hypervigilance of significant others

Thoughts of one's own death or ambivalence about living

Guilt/responsibility—assuming or assigning blame—scapegoating

Acute depression—deep sadness, uncontrolled crying, lethargy, deep sighing

Nightmares—flashbacks—posttraumatic stress

Need for validation—Is there anyone out there who knows my pain?

Embarrassment/shame/stigma

Obsessive Review—mentally visualizing steps taken toward his/her death

RECONCILIATION—Resigned—Progressing from discord to accord

Acknowledgment of death, loss and its permanence

Accepting cause of death as suicide—cause of death becomes secondary

Acquiescing to finding no definable reason—does not deter continued searching

RESUSCITATION—Effort to regain emotional equilibrium

Managing grief by expressing feelings—resuming some control—coming to terms

Regaining a measure of composure

Choosing to live

Establishing a "new normal"

RECONSTRUCTION – Adjusting to life without the deceased/mastering the grief

Reorganization—restoring orderliness in one's life

Physical readjustments—Living situation, finances, social adjustment

Reaffirming faith in God; restored trust in self, family, friends

Redefining the future

Transitioning—living presence into loving memory

RESURRECTION—Relinquishing bondage to suicide— Re-engaging in life—free to live again

Investing grief energy—making meaning and purpose

Renewed hope—my life is not over

Revived pleasure in surroundings/activities; may differ from pre-death pleasures

Shame, Silence, and Stigma

"I believe the person who commits suicide puts his psychological skeleton in the survivors closet."

Edwin Shneidman, PhD, Preface,
Survivors of Suicide, ed. Albert C. Cain

Shortly after our son's death by suicide, a friend visited with me in our home. As we sat drinking coffee at the kitchen table, she asked, "How are you dealing with the shame?" Although I had felt some embarrassment because Kent had killed himself, I was stunned by her audacity and insensitivity. My husband, reading in the adjoining room, overheard her question. He came to stand by my side, put his hand on my shoulder, looked her in the eye and said, "We aren't ashamed. We were never ashamed of Kent while he lived and we will not be shamed by his death." I do not believe she intended to be hurtful: uninformed, yes; uncaring, no.

Ignorance is the basis for shame and stigma. Immediately following a suicide, punitive societal attitudes focus on the implications of the deliberately self-inflicted death. By ending his life, the deceased has shocked, frightened, and offended society. For most members of society it is inconceivable that anyone would voluntarily relinquish what man values above all else. From lack of knowledge and from no small degree of fear for their own vulnerability, members of society have a great need to distance themselves from the one who intentionally ends his life. They may do so by condemning and diminishing the worth of that person and by judging his survivors. Censure and condemnation place an almost intolerable burden upon the survivor's shoulders, a burden of shame for the death, shame for their dead, and shame for themselves . . . the parents, spouses, children, and siblings who struggle in suicide's aftermath. This burden of condemnation and shaming is called stigma.

John was in his mid eighties when he attended our suicide bereavement support group, accompanied by his wife and daughter. John's wife expressed concern for his mental well-being. Throughout their many years of marriage John had seldom mentioned his father, but as he grew older he had begun to speak more frequently of him and the shameful way he had died. John was very open with the group about his father's suicide, which occurred when John was nine years old. John's parents had homesteaded in North Dakota and constantly battled wind, grasshoppers, and drought to keep their land. As an only child and living far from the closest neighbor, John shared a very close relationship with his father. One morning, after a lengthy season of drought and dry winds, John and his mother found his father hanging from the windmill. With the help of neighbors, his father was buried. John's mother decreed, "We will not speak of this again," and they didn't. John said, "I knew my dad had done a terrible, terrible thing and I knew we were very ashamed of it. I didn't understand how he could leave me if he loved me or why I could love and miss him so much when he had done something so bad." Throughout John's life he had been conflicted between his deep love for his father and the fact that his father had disgraced him and his mother by committing the terrible sin of ending his life.

All group participants that evening generously focused on John's loss and long-lived shame. In their own ways, all of them lovingly assured John that he needn't be ashamed of how his father died, that his father had died not from something evil or unspeakable but of depression, an illness possibly exacerbated by disillusionment, discouragement, and despair. At the meeting's end John rose from his chair, stood in the center of our grief circle with tears streaming down his face, he said, "You will never know what this means to me . . . what you've done for me. You've given my dad back to me. I am not ashamed of him, not any more. Thank you. Thank you." John never came to another meeting. He got what he needed to live out his life at peace with his father's death.

While a sense of shame and fear of judgment are by *no means the most intense emotional response* following suicide, they are often primary ones. The fact that a family member has crossed the greatest of all taboo boundaries can be a source of embarrassment. Religious connotations and age-old bias, whether from their own beliefs or imposed by others, can cause suicide-bereaved families a great amount of needless pain.

Occasionally families bereaved by suicide, fearing the impact of stigma, opt to dispose of the remains of their deceased as quickly and quietly as possible. In their initial traumatized confusion, they may even hope to keep the fact of suicide a secret, and thereby protect themselves and their dead from judgment. By denying themselves the right to publicly acknowledge the death and its cause, the bereaved forfeit solace and support from their social, work, and faith communities. By opting against burial or memorial service, they are depriving themselves of the ceremonial rituals that acknowledge a life has ended, that overwhelming emotional pain results, and that consolation is needed. Efforts at secrecy make a "hands off" statement to their communities, leaving the bereaved without the resuscitating value of comforting, sympathetic friends and the right to grieve openly.

Secrecy about the cause of death creates a distorted sense of reality within the bereaved family that encourages withdrawal and constricted expressions of grief. Secrecy can create distrust and reshuffling of family alliances that result in dissension, conflict, and further loss. Further, secrecy includes the perpetual fear of discovery and the anxiety of living a lie.

In the past, secrecy surrounding suicide was not uncommon but today we are a more enlightened society, and hopefully a more compassionate one. We know suicide is rooted in mental illness, not selfishness or cowardliness. We know mental illness can be terminal just as can cancer and heart disease. We know there is great sorrow surrounding suicide, before for the deceased and afterward for the bereaved. Suicide is not a reason for silence and shame. Suicide is a tragedy, not a disgrace.

Striving to Understand Depression

"In depression . . . faith in deliverance, in ultimate restoration, is absent. The pain is unrelenting and what makes the condition intolerable is the foreknowledge that no remedy will come—not in a day, an hour, a month or a minute. . . .it is hopelessness even more than pain that crushes the spirit."

William Styron, *Darkness Visible*

To gain some understanding of my son's state of mind before he ended his life, I spent hundreds of hours reading about depression as an illness and talking with individuals who suffer from a depressive illness. I talked with some who had seriously contemplated suicide. The understanding I gained led to some degree of reconciliation with the cause of his death. I share this understanding in the hope it will provide peace of mind to others.

It is normal to feel down or sad at times, especially following disappointments or negative life events. Clinical depression is much more than sadness or the blues. It is a serious illness or condition that limits the ability to feel good and function normally. It can be deep and prolonged, lasting for months, even years. Depression has been described as "being in a deep, black pit," as days of "hanging from a cliff by my fingertips," having a sense of worthlessness, hopelessness, and impending doom, being unable to help oneself, and not knowing this state of mind can be helped. Some deeply depressed individuals do not recognize their suffering as a mental disorder; they only know they are in tremendous emotional pain.

Each of the several types of depression has unique symptoms, causes, and effects. Each type is diagnosable and treatable. Major depression is characterized by a persistent sad mood, feelings of worthlessness or guilt, and the inability to experience happiness. Symptoms of major depression interfere with normal functioning and coping abilities and can range from moderate to severe. Without treatment major depression can last several months. Some victims of major depression suffer a single episode, but most commonly, major depression is a recurring disorder.

Dysthymia, recurrent, mild depression, is chronic "low-grade" depression. Although symptoms of dysthymia are not as painful or debilitating as major depression, they can last many months. Sufferers may think what they are experiencing is normal, the way everyone feels.

Seasonal Affective Disorder (SAD) is a pattern of seasonal depression linked to gloomy, rainy or overcast days and little sunlight. Sufferers tend to withdraw socially, may seem lethargic, and need lots of sleep. Treatment usually involves therapy using artificial light.

Bipolar disorder, also known as manic depression, is characterized by cycling mood changes alternating between the extreme lows of major depression and manic episodes of extreme, almost euphoric, highs, featuring hyperactive, impulsive behavior. The treatment for bipolar disorder usually differs considerably from other types of depression.[1]

According to the U.S. Preventive Services Task Force, more than 90 percent of people who complete suicide had a mental disorder, such as depression, substance abuse, or both. Depression is seldom caused by one event or reason, but is the often the result of a buildup of several factors with causes varying from person to person. It is a serious illness that can

---

[1] *Disclaimer. Descriptions of depression herein are not to be interpreted as professional diagnosis or advice. If you are concerned about your own depression or that of another person, immediately make an appointment to see a mental health professional or your primary care physician or go to the emergency room of the nearest hospital and ask for help.*

be caused when neurotransmitters (chemicals that carry signals through the nervous system) get out of balance or become disrupted in some way. A significant life event—the death of a loved one, a divorce, loss of a body part, loss of status or reputation, job loss, moving to a new area, or a breakup with a spouse, partner, boyfriend, or girlfriend— can bring on symptoms of depression. Physical, mental, emotional, and sexual abuse can be an underlying cause of depression. Stress can be a factor. Chronic illness can contribute to clinical depression. Addiction can be a factor, especially when drugs or alcohol are used by depressed individuals to relieve or mask the pain of depression. Genetics may be involved, for depression tends to run in families, although suicide is not genetic.

Often those closest to the depressed individual have no awareness that their family member or friend is suffering from depression. Even a deeply depressed person can be quite adept at masking depression, putting on a happy face, going through the motions of being in control and living well. Personality and behavior changes symptomatic of depression can be subtle and progress slowly, which can make it harder for family members to notice changes.

Depression is not always an illness of long duration. Situational depression can occur when an individual suffers an acute loss or is involved in a crime or other inappropriate activity, causing them to feel trapped and without options. In these cases the suicide may be a spontaneous or impulsive act, with no risk indicators present.

Although I knew my son was depressed after an illness caused him to lose a semester's college tuition, and a poor economy made jobs very difficult to find, I didn't know he could become suicidal. I didn't even know depression was a serious illness. I now understand depressive illness as a closed, cold, isolated, impregnable world, so dark, so crushing and all-consuming that it blinds the depressed individual to all but the need to be free of it.

I believe my son struggled to live. The note he left to us said, "I've tried. I just can't make it. I guess I'm just not worth it." I have often pondered the meaning of "it." Was "it" the ability to feel happiness, to feel worthy and valuable? Was "it" his struggle to overcome needs, thoughts, and feelings he didn't understand and thought he never would? Kent knew he was dearly loved by his family and deeply loved each of us in return. If loving and being loved kept people from ending their life, there would be very few suicides. Love has little to do with suicide. Emotional pain perceived by the sufferer as intolerable, irresolvable, and unending has everything to do with it.

Jane, survivor of her son, Matthew, who ended his life at age eighteen, shares in a suicide survivor support group what she believes it is like to be in a severely depressed state.

"Imagine yourself in a mirrored box; the ceiling, the floor, and four walls are all mirrored. You feel trapped, frightened, and overwhelmed. You are in great emotional pain; from every direction your misery is reflected back to you, distorted and magnified, like a fun-house mirror. The box becomes increasingly confining. You struggle to find a more comfortable point of view or to free yourself. You find none and you can find no way out. Outside the mirrored box are family and friends, people who love you, willing to help. You can't hear them, you can't see them or feel their concern. And they do not, cannot see your situation as you see it. As you look in each direction, your sense of helplessness grows, consuming your strength and ability to cope. There seems to be no hope of relief from the continuous reflections of your unrelenting pain. You believe you cannot endure it another day, hour, minute. Very possibly, at this point, ending your life looks like the only remaining option, the only escape from the mirrored box."

From the perception of a person deeply depressed and in such pain that he thinks of ending his life, everything that happens reinforces the distorted view that there is no hope, help, or alternative. Ending one's life becomes the only escape. It is difficult for those left behind to understand a suicidal person's perspective because the survivor views the inside of the box from a rational state of mind. The suicidal person does not.

ENLIGHTENING PIECES

Coping on a Different Psychological Level

"Death by suicide is not a gentle deathbed gathering; it rips apart lives and beliefs, and sets its survivors on a prolonged and devastating journey."

Kay Redfield Jamison, *Night Falls Fast*

Grief following suicide is multifaceted and compounded. Every emotional response, every dimension and layer of grief is singularly affected, complicated, distorted, and magnified by the fact of suicide. Suicide bereaved grieve the death of one dearly loved; they grieve as well the cause of that death, the fact of suicide, and everything suicide means—and all an uninformed, often judgmental, society believes suicide to mean.

MaryAnn was on the East Coast caring for her terminally ill mother when she received tragic news. The elder of her two sons, twenty-two-year-old Jerry, had died in a hunting accident. She found solace in the large number of friends who attended his funeral. A few weeks following Jerry's death, one of his former teachers approached MaryAnn at a supermarket and inquired of her well-being. The teacher's final comment was, "Jerry was the last person I'd have thought would commit suicide." In shock, MaryAnn somehow made her way home. "I knew immediately what he had said was true. All of my ignored and unanswered questions suddenly made sense. I confronted my husband and my surviving son. They admitted Jerry had died by his own hand. They had hoped to protect me by letting me believe it was an accident."MaryAnn said, "I had mourned Jerry for weeks, believing he had left our family and this life against his will, when, in fact, he had intentionally left. I had found comfort from expressions of sympathy from so many people who all the time had known what I did not . . . that Jerry had killed himself. I felt betrayed, foolish, and embarrassed. I was so very angry at my husband and son! They had left me behind. They had had those weeks to accept and cope with Jerry's death as suicide while I was right back at square one. Little by little I was beginning to cope with Jerry's death, but when I learned he had killed himself it was as if it had just happened and I had to start grieving from the beginning— only my feelings were very, very different. I was terribly grieved by Jerry's accidental death but mourned him lovingly. But I mourned Jerry's suicide in conflict with him, absolutely enraged by what he had done. I put away all his pictures and wouldn't talk about him or say his name for a very long time. I guess I was trying to punish him for leaving us, for killing himself."

Comforted by the motive of her husband and surviving son, MaryAnn resolved the conflict with them fairly quickly. It took longer for her to grow through her anger at her dead son. In the years since Jerry's death MaryAnn has reconciled to suicide as the cause of his death. When the need arises she does what she once thought impossible: speaks openly of her own experience to comfort others who have lost a loved one through suicide. MaryAnn believes that in spite of the indescribable pain of acknowledging suicide as the cause of a loved one's death, there is great benefit from openly and freely grieving the cause of the death as well as the fact of the death from the time the death occurs.

When maiming is involved

From the time Sam was diagnosed as bipolar at age sixteen until he died at eighteen years of age, he was treated with several medications and therapy. During a hospitalization Sam said he hated being there and asked what he needed to do or say to be released. Thereafter, he wore a mask of well-being that disarmed his caregivers, causing them to disregard some concerns expressed by his mother, Gwen, a nurse.

In March 2004, during a disagreement with his girlfriend, Sam shot her in the face. He then went to his home, changed his clothes, called his mother, disclosing nothing of what had taken place, and drove to a deserted country road, where he shot and killed himself. This tragedy occurred the day after the fourth birthday of Sam's little brother, Abe.

The anguish of Sam's mother, stepfather, and two young half-siblings was embraced and supported by their church family. The entire small community, grieving the loss of this bright, popular young man, extended reinforcement to the family. The community supported the family of Sam's girlfriend as well. Soon after the tragedy Gwen called on the injured girl to express her sorrow and concern. The girl lost an eye in the shooting and although she must have been devastated Sam's family has never been aware of any animosity expressed toward them by her or her family.

Each member of Sam's surviving family participated in weekly therapy for nearly a year. Sam's stepfather, Trent, tells of a session during which Sam's mother sat sobbing uncontrollably and he expressed his concern for the depth of her despair to the therapist. The therapist told him Gwen's response was normal but that he was deeply concerned for Trent, who didn't express his pain. Trent believed he needed to control his feelings and be strong for Sam's mother and their young children. After the therapist gave him permission and encouragement to grieve openly Trent said it was as if the lid had been lifted from a violently boiling kettle. He allowed himself to express his grief and his healing began.

Gwen and Trent believe the coping techniques they learned in counseling and the hard work of mourning as a family has laid a foundation for a healthy future. Sam's sister, Faith, now fourteen, and Abe, nearly twelve, share some of their loss experience in the chapter of this book entitled Suicide Bereaved Children.

A heartbreaking note: In the days immediately following Sam's suicide the Federal Drug Administration released a warning that certain drugs prescribed for mental illness could have adverse effect on teens, even leading to suicide. A drug Sam had been taking was on the warning list.

Grieving accidental, natural, and suicidal deaths

Ralph, a retired air force colonel, and his wife, Donna, raised three sons. The middle son was killed a few hours following his college graduation when the motorcycle he was riding collided with a truck. The youngest son deliberately asphyxiated himself following ridicule and rejection by a married woman with whom he had a brief affair. The last and oldest son, a military officer, died of a heart attack as he jogged after hours while on a tour of duty.

The initial tragedy, the accidental death of their middle son, was deeply grieved. He was a brilliant young man with a promising future. It was an unexpected, violent death. Donna and Ralph were devastated. Messages of condolence from military friends around the world comforted them. Many parents who had lost a child offered empathy and encouragement. Ralph and Donna found hope by hearing how others coped and that life could be satisfying and joyous again.

Three years later, the youngest son, also in his early twenties, became involved with an older woman, a doctor's wife, who flattered him with suggestions he was so virile and attractive that she wanted to be with him permanently. Donna was very concerned when her son shared his dream that this woman would divorce her husband and marry him. She knew her son to be socially immature and without means to provide the woman's accustomed lifestyle. She was concerned by the fifteen-year age difference and the social status the woman enjoyed as a physician's wife. Donna suggested to him that if the woman was serious, it would be wise for him to wait until she was free before he committed to the relationship. When her son approached his lover about divorcing her husband to marry him she laughed, told him that divorce and marriage were never a consideration, and that their affair was just a "fun thing."

That evening, before he left for work, he told Donna of the rejection. Early the next morning he was found in his car, dead by asphyxiation. Donna and Ralph's grief was very different from their grief after the first son died. Donna bitterly blamed the woman for using her son and expressing no remorse for his death. Donna's very strict Catholic convent schooling created many pitfalls in her grief journey. Her grief was compounded by her surviving son's wife, who expressed her belief that it would place Donna and Ralph's only grandchildren at risk of suicide to accept their deceased uncle's record collection or to have further contact with Donna and Ralph. While the surviving son visited them on a regular basis, they were not permitted interaction with their grandchildren. Their messages of congratulations for scholastic accomplishment were unanswered and gifts unacknowledged.

The third and last of Ralph and Donna's three sons, an air force officer, died of a heart attack while jogging after work during short-term duty at a foreign base. Donna spoke of the differences in mourning the three son's deaths. The first death was accidental, perhaps the result of carelessness, but no blame was placed. Donna and Ralph had been powerless over what happened. While they were heartbroken, they had the comfort and reassurance of other parents that they would be able to endure the pain and loss. The heart attack, too, was beyond their control, a natural death, albeit sudden and unexpected. But the suicide was a death Donna felt could have been prevented. Donna agonized over her perceived guilt and neglect in not being more firm in cautioning her son about his infatuation. Their grief was complicated by terrible frustration and anger toward someone they believed contributed to his death. The consequences created by the separation mandated by their grandchildren's mother caused further losses that deprived them of ongoing family support and hope for pleasure and joy in the future. Ralph and Donna coped by finding a focus for their physical energy and that allowed space for processing their emotional responses. Upon military retirement Ralph had formed a real estate company. Following the first son's death they focused on building a house, doing all the planning and much of the work themselves. Following the second son's death they built another house, and Donna meticulously finished all the woodwork. After the oldest son died, in spite of age and health problems, they designed, built, and traveled to Denmark to buy furnishings for a third house. For Donna and Ralph, keeping their minds and hands very busy was a means of coping and healing.

There are levels of coping during suicide bereavement not demanded of grievers of other causes of death. Some researchers indicate that grief after suicide takes no longer to work through than grief for other causes of death. I neither refute nor agree with such findings, but my personal experience suggests that, since bereaved by suicide carry a double burden, grief for the death and for the cause of death, they must work much harder if they are to achieve resolution within the same time frame.

Is Suicide a Choice?

*"Our God has given us free will.
And with that free will comes the burden of choice."*

ColleenMcCullough, *The Thornbirds,*

A reminder: The chapter About Suicide references Edwin Shneidman's *The Suicidal Mind,* where he defines the commonalities of suicide and points out that the common purpose of suicide is to seek a solution. The goal of suicide is cessation of consciousness to stop unendurable pain.

The choice implied by suicide is an assault on every aspect of the survivors' existence; upon their relationships with the one who has died; upon their views of themselves and upon their belief systems. The choice implied by a loved one's deliberate self-destruction causes the survivors to focus obsessively on the role they played in the loved one's decision and often, specifically, the role they may believe they should have played and didn't. The choice implied by the act of killing oneself lays bare for society's judgment the worth of the person who made the choice and the value of the relationships they shared. It brings into question the strength of character of one who would reject what others enjoy, value, and protect above all else: their life.

But is suicide a choice? Or did the individual who ended his/her life believe, at that time, there was no other way to find relief and peace? Was it their choice to be gone from this life, from loved ones, or was it an act born of a desperate need to be free of emotional pain they perceived as endless, unrelenting, and irresolvable? Pain so overwhelming and persistent they were blinded to other options?

Following my son's suicide I was greatly conflicted over the issue of choice. It was beyond my comprehension that this cherished young man, who loved his family and appeared to love living, would choose to leave us by deliberately ending his own life. His "choice" was contrary to everything he had been taught and that we thought he believed. It was not until I began to study the vast variability of human behavior, and especially suicide, that I had an inkling of how difficult and painful "choice" had been for him. I think the grief he felt from believing he had no other choice accounted for the still-damp tears my fingers traced across his cheek as I knelt by his side while waiting for the ambulance.

At a suicidology conference a number of years ago I made the acquaintance of a young man who had attempted to end his life. He eloquently articulated the pain of living; of going through the motions every day, from the time his feet hit the floor in the morning until he crawled into bed at night, trying to keep at bay the overwhelming pain he felt whenever he was quiet. He told of faking well-being, pleasantries, and joviality. He told of the extreme effort to face his fellow employees and his family each day. Finally, he became so exhausted from pretense that he cared less and less about pretending. As the pain of living grew more intense and his future seemed more hopeless, he planned how he could end his life. One morning he awoke with a greater sense of dread and hopelessness than ever before. He opened his pill stash and swallowed one handful after another.

He awakened in a hospital ICU on a respirator. His life was saved when his brother stopped to wish their mother a Happy Mother's Day and found him. As a result, depression was diagnosed, treatment begun, and his sense of well-being and control eventually restored. He had come to tell others of his choice, his near death, and his revived love of life. When I asked him why he had chosen Mother's Day of all days he answered, "I was totally oblivious to what day it was when I swallowed those pills. I just knew I could not face another hour of living with my pain." He realized that had he died that day his mother might have forever perceived his death as a message of complete rejection.

As survivors mourning the suicide of someone dear, we must not assume responsibility for the "choice" they made, the decision they reached, the option they exercised, or the death they left their loved ones to mourn. They were struggling with demons we could not see, with pain they could not articulate, perhaps the torment of an undiagnosed mental illness or being trapped in an irreconcilable situation. They experienced despair so intense it crowded out their love of living, despair that grew far greater than their fear of dying and leaving those they loved. One's last breath is valued above all else. An individual who kills him/herself does not give up that last breath easily, not without searching for, failing to find, and finally perceiving there were no other options. In their distorted perception, at least for a small space of time, there was no other way. Regardless of how impulsive, preventable, and regrettable we believe the choice to have been, the death that resulted from exercising that option, making that choice is our loved one's responsibility.

Is Suicide a Selfish and Cowardly Act?

*"Oh, great and just God, no man among us knows what the
sleeper knows, nor is it for us to judge what lies between him
and Thee."*

Willa Cather, *My Antonia*

Comments overheard by suicide survivors that suicide is a
selfish and cowardly act create a sense of shame, a loss of dignity, and feeling deprived of the right to grieve. Thoughtless
remarks may be made by first respondents to the death scene,
by medical personnel in the emergency room, by friends gathering in support of the family, even by a family member fumbling
for a reason or cause for the death. The primary survivor may
internalize a derogatory statement as an assault on the character of the one who died and, thus, an assault upon themselves.
They may feel anger, embarrassment, and a need to defend their
loved one. It would not be unusual for the survivor to remain
silent because she can think of no response, no justification or
defense to counteract the label cowardly or selfish, nor would
it be surprising for a survivor to be too numb and emotionally
exhausted to make a stand even if a response came to mind.

Is suicide a cowardly act?

Many people who have deliberately ended their lives, even
those who died quite young, exhibited strength, tenacity, and
courage throughout their lives and would never have been defined as cowardly had they continued to live or had they died
in another manner. Is it fair, then, that the character of one who
ends his/her own life is diminished, defamed, and defined by a
final desperate act? by society's perpetuation of an unfounded
aphorism? by the need of others to distance themselves from

the act of suicide by labeling the individual who ends his/her life as a coward? For an individual to give up what man values above all else is not done without struggle, without regret, without pain. Suicide is an act born of desperation, often rooted in the pain of mental illness, not cowardice.

Is killing oneself an act of selfishness?

Or do thoughts of suicide radiate from the pain-filled core of an individual's being, eroding self-esteem, distorting rational thought, blinding the sufferer to love of family, the joy of living, and viable options? Does depression extinguish hope, love of self and life until all that remains is the engulfing quicksand of psychic pain perceived by the individual as unbearable, unrelenting, and irresolvable?

There are situations where an individual ends his/her life with a distorted perception that the family will function better or be happier without him/her; that once he/she is gone taking his/her problems with him/her the family will return to some sense of normalcy. This is the suicidal individual's distorted perception and not a fact. In another scenario, the perception of someone who has committed a crime prior to ending his/her life may be to protect the surviving family or him/herself from shame and punishment.

Without oversimplifying the complexity of the suicidal state of mind, I want to suggest survivors regard the act of suicide as a result of their loved one being helplessly immobilized by their mental/emotional pain, totally absorbed, trapped, inert, overwhelmed, without hope, and in desperate need of relief. Seeking relief in death does not translate as a wish to be dead, but rather as a need to be free of pain. It has been said that suicide occurs when all other means of coping have been exhausted, when the pain of living has grown greater than the fear of dying.

As hurtful as it will be for bereaved left to struggle with the added dimension of unawareness of their loved one's conflict, there may also be a bit of comfort in recognizing the similarity of the powerlessness of grief to the pre-suicide state of mind. The isolated, pain-consumed world that precedes suicide cannot be entirely dissimilar to the grief suicide bereaved experience following the death. The great difference is that persons bereaved by suicide know what they have lost, they know why they grieve, why they feel depressed, out of control, and overwhelmed. Very possibly, in contrast, the suicidal individual did not understand why he or she was depressed and felt out of control and overwhelmed. The bereaved can give expression to their pain and receive solace for their grief. They can even grasp the concept of a future when they won't hurt so badly. Most likely, the suicidal individual could not.

The pain-focused self-centeredness that precedes suicide differs greatly and is far more complex than the superficial, denigrating dismissal of suicide as a selfish act, caring too much for oneself and too little for others. While the act of suicide may grow from the center of a hopeless, grief-absorbed being, is it the result of selfishness? Or is it the result of psychic pain that may have gone unrecognized, untended, and unjustly labeled? Can we understand it as a grief that precedes suicide?

Religious Reflections on Suicide

"When I behold any soul in agony, who had thought of Me with pleasure, or who had performed any works deserving of reward, I appear to that soul at the moment of death, with a countenance so full of love and mercy, that the soul repents from its inmost depths for having offended Me, and that soul is saved by this repentance."

St. Gertrude, *Legatus Divinae Pietatis*

My early religious education planted the seed of belief that those who usurp God's wisdom and power by intentionally ending their life are doomed to spend eternity in the fiery furnaces of hell. That seed lay dormant to erupt the day my son killed himself into a grasping, smothering entanglement of doubt and fear for his immortal soul.

The clergy who responded the day of our son's death offered no consolation to my plea for reassurance that God had not slammed the gates of Heaven in the face of my approaching child. Rather, they quoted discomforting scripture and dogma that seemed to reinforce a condemning, avenging God—a God who would, indeed, turn my son away.

This placed my deep-rooted faith in conflict with the myopic bias of these clergy. I was left with this choice: to turn away from God, their damning, denying God, or to rely upon my own belief and trust in an all-knowing, all-loving, all-forgiving almighty; my God, who had known my son's state of mind, my God, who had offered my son other choices but forgave the choice he made.

Many months following my son's death, as I researched religious reflections on suicide, I came across *Sitting By My Laughing Fire* and the words of Ruth Bell Graham as she offered comfort to a mother who had lost a son through suicide, "God did not call your loved one Home, but He welcomed them with open arms." Oh! The anguish I would have been spared had I read this in the early days of my bereavement.

The ability of suicide bereaved to make adjustment to their loss is often impeded and complicated by additional losses related to faith. Betty shared her sorrow for the loss of her church home and her once-safe faith environment. She spoke of her sense of betrayal at what she believed to be misrepresentation of God's laws by her pastor and her loss of hope at being stripped of her religious identity. Her pain was palpable as she spoke of her sense of responsibility following her husband's suicide.

Betty's husband, Ben, was an alcoholic. His drinking had caused considerable deprivation, humiliation, and conflict for Betty and her young family, who lived in a small, rural community. She sought strength and refuge by increasing her devotion to God in a fundamentalist church. She confided to her pastor the pain her husband's drinking caused the family. Telling her that Ben's love of liquor was a tool of the devil, who was wrestling with God for control of her husband's soul, the pastor advised her to exert unrelenting effort to save that soul for God.

Betty attended Bible study and prayer meetings several times a week. She spent hours, sometimes far into the night, praying for and with her husband in an effort to convince him to accept salvation and to be forever rid of his need for alcohol. "He tried, he really tried," Betty said. Ben attended church services and took part in daily family devotions, and for weeks there was no drinking. She praised the Lord that they were winning the battle over drink and the devil.

Then, with the failure of their struggling business, they fell deeper into debt and Ben retreated to the bottle. He told her how sorry he was for having failed and spoke of his wretchedness at being such a poor husband, father, and provider. Betty confided her husband's lament to her pastor, and again the pastor admonished her to increase her prayerful effort to rescue her husband's soul from the devil.

One Sunday after church, following the noon meal, Betty and Ben lay down to rest, as was their custom. She turned on her side, her back to Ben, reached for her Bible, and began to read to him of repentance and forgiveness. She heard the nightstand drawer open, followed by a click, and turned in time to see him put a bullet through his head.

During her husband's funeral the pastor directed few words of comfort toward Betty and her children. Instead, he reviled the poor, pitiful, lost souls who, by ending their own life, deprived themselves of Heaven, of the presence of God, and of reunion in Glory with their loved ones. He spoke of Satan at work in their midst and the need to cast him out.

Betty said, "I was stunned and heart-sickened by his words. I watched in disbelief as the congregation physically drew away from us as if they feared being contaminated." Thereafter Betty was almost totally bereft of support from the community. Ben's family blamed her for "driving him to kill himself." One member of the family even suggested to others in the community that Betty may have been the killer. Betty's oldest daughter separated herself from the family, a breach that never healed. The once-safe community grew so threatening and uncomfortable it was necessary for Betty and her three younger children to relocate.

"I was raised in these beliefs," Betty said. "They were all I knew. I never questioned them, but now I am forced to re-evaluate my faith. I know God is still in me and my trust is in Him. Someday I hope to find a church where I can safely place my trust and serve again." She concluded her heartbroken musings with her belated understanding, gained from attending Al-Anon meetings; Ben had suffered from a disease, not from evil. She expressed her belief that he had been a victim. "We were both victims," she said, "of ignorance, intolerance, and self-righteousness."

Historically, suicide has been viewed as a sin by nearly all religions. However, the centuries-old laws regarding suicide that continue to be worrisome and hurtful to modern-day suicide bereaved have a foundation in early Christianity. Jesus told His followers of a utopian afterlife, free of earthly trials and tribulation. Early Christian martyrs, struggling against extremely hard times, began ending their lives to reach the promised paradise. In the fourth century A. D., suicide had become so prevalent that tax losses due to suicide became a problem to the government treasury. To stop the rash of suicides, St. Augustine codified the Church's official disapproval of suicide by placing it in a moral framework and condemning it as a grievous sin.

In the thirteenth century, in *Summa Theologica*, Thomas Aquinas further specified the Church's attitude toward suicide when he condemned suicide as unnatural and a usurpation of God's power. To discourage people from ending their lives, very harsh judgment and retribution were directed toward the surviving family of a suicide. During the Middle Ages anyone attempting to end his life was punished by flogging and imprisonment and was stripped of all social and financial assets. The body of a suicide was buried at a crossroads with a spike driven through the heart and stones piled upon the grave, or the corpse was dragged through the village streets, desecrated, and displayed in the village square. The property of a suicide and that of his family were confiscated by the government, leaving the surviving families to live as destitute outcasts. Aquinas's writings became the center of Christian doctrine, although he took many of his arguments from Plato and Aristotle, not from the Bible.

The only Biblical authority is the interpretation of the sixth commandment, "Thou shalt not kill." Seven suicides are mentioned in the Holy Bible: Abimelich (Judges), Samson (Judges), Saul and his armor bearer (Samuel), Achitophel (Samuel), and Zimri (I Kings) in the Old Testament and, of course, Judas Iscariot (Matthew) in the New Testament. There is no condemnation of any of them.

In the early 1960's, the Vatican changed the code of canon law. Catholics who took their own lives would no longer be denied a Catholic funeral or burial in a Catholic cemetery. *Religion & Ethics Newsweekly*, October 21, 2005, quotes a response to this change by Father Charles Rubey, Chicago Catholic Charities and director of Loving Outreach to Survivors of Suicide, "They took the whole issue of suicide out of the moral realm and placed it in the medical realm, where it belongs."

The contemporary religious scene comprises a broad variance in interpretation. Not all theological perspective about suicide is judgmental and condemning. More frequently clergy are offering comfort and hope to families bereaved by suicide. Survivors in recent years, more often than not, tell of the great strength and support given by their clergy and express sympathy and concern for survivors who have had negative responses from their faith-based community. Father Rubey explains, "Suicide happens because people are in extraordinary pain. The person who completes suicide is saying, 'I can no longer handle the pain in my life.' Suicide is not about religion. It's not about morality. It's about pain."

Father Joe, a Catholic priest in my city, officiated at the funeral of his thirty-year-old nephew who had completed suicide. Although Father Joe had tended numerous families following suicide, this death in his own family caused him to reassess his understanding of suicide bereavement and to admit limits in ministering to survivors. He attended our support group as a survivor to mourn with others but also to gain insight into the healing needs of suicide bereaved. Father Joe, Father Rubey, and Rabbi Earl Grollman, who writes extensively about the issue of suicide, exemplify increasing awareness and sensitivity by faith-based leaders toward persons who end their lives and those who survive them.

The purity of belief expressed by a middle-aged seminary student who is also a suicide-bereaved mother echoes the words of St. Gertrude that offer great comfort to those seeking answers regarding salvation, "God communicates spirit to spirit. Man doesn't have to be conscious for God to accept the soul's request for salvation or forgiveness. The body dies ... the soul lives forever."

My agonizing search for God's acceptance of my son, even though he ended his own life, strengthened my faith and brought me peace. What I found assured me that God did not turn my son away because of how he died. Most certainly, God opened His arms, embraced my son, and welcomed him Home because of how he lived.

Phantom Pain

*"Those we love are with the Lord, and the Lord has promised
to be with us. If they are with Him, and He is with us,
they cannot be far away."*

Peter Marshall, *Mr. Jones, Meet the Master*

Just before Christmas, four months after the suicide of my son, Kent, I was in a department store going about the heart-heavy business of selecting gifts for my surviving family. A movement caught my eye. I glanced up and thought I saw Kent standing at a counter a few aisles away. My heart did a drum roll. I rushed toward the spot where I had seen him. I blinked and looked again. He was gone. In his place, conversing with a sales lady was a tall, dark-headed young man who somewhat resembled Kent. I was overcome with sorrow and yearning. Kent loved Christmas. He was always full of excitement, anticipation, secrets, and surprises. Although reason reminded me Kent was dead, that I had not really seen him, my heart and mind protested, for neither had yet reconciled to the fact that he was forever beyond my sight, touch, and hearing.

One surviving mother told of standing at a front window on an autumn evening a few weeks following her son's death and seeing the back of a boy wearing a jacket similar to her son's, riding a bicycle down the street away from her. In that instant she recognized the rider as her son Jamie. She ran out the front door and down the street after him shouting, "Jamie! Jamie! Stop, Jamie!" She caught up with the rider and as she reached for the bike's back fender to stop him the boy turned, wide-eyed, his face full of fear, and he said, "What's the matter with you lady? Are you crazy?" She said, "I was. I was crazy with grief, missing, and longing."

A surviving widow told of a pickup truck in her small community that was the same make, model, and color as the one driven by her deceased husband. The pickup owner wore a cowboy hat tipped to the back of his head as he drove, just as her husband had. For months after her husband's suicide, whenever she saw that pickup drive by, for an instant she experienced a surge of expectation that her husband was behind the wheel and was coming home to her.

Many survivors share similar experiences, often asking if this is a normal reaction to losing a loved one to suicide. I believe it is a reaction common for *all* who suffer the loss of a loved one, regardless of cause, but especially a sudden death. I call this experience of seeing, feeling, or sensing the presence of our loved one *phantom pain.*

Phantom pain refers to the sensation experienced by persons who have had a limb amputated yet continue to have feeling in the missing appendage. The amputee may complain his foot itches, his leg is cold, his fingers are cramped; some experience severe, piercing pain. This pain is very real. The area of the brain originally representing the missing limb remains functional even though the limb no longer exists. Stimulation of this area of the brain or of the body area close to the amputation results in sensation as if the limb were still attached. With treatment and time, phantom pain usually becomes less frequent and severe, although the amputation site will likely always remain tender, needing of care and subject to stimuli.

When a loved one dies suddenly, our psyche is shocked, traumatized by the abrupt severing of the relationship. The part of the brain connected to that relationship remains functional even though the physical connection has been broken by death. In the months following the death of someone close, it is not at all unusual to think we see them, especially when there is a trigger to stimulate that reaction. For me, Christmas time was the stimulus. That reminder causes us to see, hear, smell, or feel the presence of the one who has died. We aren't losing our mind. We are grieving the permanent separation from a part of our own life. We are experiencing phantom pain, a reminder of what once was a beloved part of our physical life even as the amputation site is toughening, scarring, and strengthening.

Although we suffer, we are healing. Healing allows the raw emotional wound to close, scar and strengthen in order to bear the weight of the loss and better tolerate abrasions, bumps, reminders, and stimuli. Healing involves reconciling to the severing, the loss, the amputation. Healing is adjusting our emotional, spiritual, and physical self to function without the part that has been lost. Healing is adapting to living with and beyond the imbalance created by the loss. We don't like it! But we have to adapt to it, and we can. Over time, the raging, all-consuming pain resulting from the amputation subsides and finally is transformed into sorrow and regret that are tolerable. But the scar resulting from the severed relationship will likely remain forever sensitive and in need of soothing.

Flashbacks

"What happened in the past that was painful has a great deal to do with what we are today, but revisiting this painful past contributes little or nothing to what we need to do now."

William Glasser, *The Choice Theory*

Flashbacks are involuntary recurrent memories of an event. They feel as if the affected individual is re-experiencing the past event. Among the most disturbing are flashbacks of traumatic events. The trauma may be magnified for those who witness the self-inflicted death or find the remains after a loved one has ended their life.

Trauma, from a Greek word meaning wound, results from events that are intolerable to feel and know. Persons who saw the suicide occur, heard the fatal shot, or found their loved one mutilated will be traumatized. Occasionally bereaved who have not viewed the scene but have imagined it or have heard it described suffer vicarious trauma. It is as if that moment in time is frozen in the mind and an out-of-control movie or loop tape repeatedly plays the scene and its impact. Trauma causes the emotional brain to reset to fight for survival because it still feels endangered. These unbidden replays, or flashbacks, intrude during waking hours and, not uncommonly, in the form of nightmares. The replayed image can cause the survivor to feel traumatized again and again, shocked and horrified by what was seen, heard, smelled or touched. Dr. Bessel van der Kolk, founder of the Trauma Center in Brookline, Mass., describes this state as the brain being stuck in a state of emergency.

Upon finding our son gut-shot on the floor, I knelt by his side waiting for the ambulance. Vivid recall of that scene plagued me for months, especially at night. The flashbacks were often triggered by a loud noise and caused me to feel anxious, fearful; my heart would pound, and I felt as if I was suffocating. I learned that deep breathing relaxed and calmed me at these times; inhaling deeply, then exhaling slowly, through my mouth. I often made a moaning, almost sobbing sound, as I did so. It was if the moaning was pain leaving my body.

Flashbacks are very disruptive and frightening. I had to find a way to prevent or redirect the replay of the bad tape when it began to play by inserting something pleasant. I took walks and sat swinging for hours on the neighborhood school playground. I found some diversion from the armloads of books I carried home from the library every few days. Historical novels and biographies held my attention for tiny spaces of time and gave me something else to focus on. When scenes of my tragedy began to replay, I would pick up a book I'd been reading and direct as much attention as I could muster to the story. I watched reruns of *I Love Lucy* or old movie comedies or musicals when I needed to eject the flashback. I avoided movies, books, or television shows with themes of violence or death, knowing they would not be helpful.

I quickly learned that recalling happy times with my son before his death did not offer needed distraction because he was in the picture. Later in my grief journey, these memories gave me great comfort. In the chapter Family Retreat, I share how helpful it was for me to have a three-day Labor Day mountain getaway with my husband, our three surviving sons, our daughter and her husband to redirect my thinking when the flashback occurred. The weekend had been planned long before our son's death, the effort it took to make the trip immediately following his burial was supreme, but it was the healthiest action our family could have taken.

Since the late 1970s when I struggled with flashbacks of my son's death scene, research regarding trauma has produced a much broader understanding of how the brain reacts to horrific events. Trauma experts such as Dr. Bessel van der Kolk explain that trauma victims need to feel safe and that a posture of calm and peace is very important to gaining internal calm and peacefulness. Some basic soothing techniques like rocking, holding, and deep breathing are calming. Rocking is not just for babies. Rock yourself. Holding someone close and being held is soothing. Breathe, inhale deeply, lifting the shoulders so the lungs can fill completely, then exhale slowly. These exercises can help calm you. Pets can play a huge role in helping us cope with trauma. It's difficult to remain agitated while stroking an animal. Being seated comfortably and watching an aquarium of fish or birds at a feeder can relax the body and free the mind. These practices also lower blood pressure and regulate breathing.

My husband returned to work less than a week after our son's funeral to distract himself by concentrating on client needs, but his sleep was sporadic and restless. After a friend invited him to play racquetball he slept soundly for the first time following Kent's death. The next day he joined the racquet club and played two or three times a week, long after he needed it to cope with sleeplessness. Exercise, especially when it demands concentration, helps reorganize the brain as well as releasing chemicals that enhance one's sense of well-being.

Martial arts are about posture, exercise, and concentration. Yoga involves posture, strengthening the body, and meditation, all of which contribute to inner peace. And do not underestimate the power of prayer when striving to calm your mind and body.

When flashbacks interrupt mourning, rob the sufferer of sleep, or continue for several months, seek professional help. A trauma treatment that suicide bereaved have found effective in confronting horrific images is a form of psychotherapy called EMDR (Eye Movement Desensitization and Reprocessing). EMDR was developed to resolve symptoms resulting from disturbing and unresolved life experiences such as assault, rape, and battlefield experiences. The therapy does not destroy the images but aids the brain in assimilating them. One of the unusual features of EMDR is that the patient does not have to discuss any of his disturbing memories in detail. The goal of EMDR therapy is to leave the patient with the emotions, understanding, and perspective that will lead to healthy and useful behaviors and interactions. EMDR is not hypnosis although the treatment resembles hypnosis because the therapist may use tapping on the patient's knees or shoulders or swing an object, such as a pencil, from side to side before the patient's eyes. To learn more about EMDR search the Internet or find an EMDR-trained therapist in the telephone directory.

It took time and experimenting with many techniques for me to learn the most effective way to manage the flashbacks to my son's death scene. In the beginning the flashbacks were frequent and very disturbing; eventually, they came less often and less vividly. There was a time when I had no control over the replay of what I saw and felt as I knelt by my son's side waiting for the ambulance. Now that scene rests in my memory and replays only if I choose to recall it.

Children Bereaved by Suicide

"Children will tell you of bruised and broken knees but have no words for their bruised and broken hearts."

Michelle Linn-Gust and John Peters, *A Winding Road*

Young children are a primary concern following the suicide of someone close, especially a parent or another adult to whom the child was close. The first inclination may be to protect children from the facts surrounding the death by being evasive or distorting the truth. To tell the surviving child other than the truth lays a foundation of distrust that may compromise their trust for a long time. Yet to tell them too much too soon can also have a negative effect.

Children deserve to have their questions answered truthfully and *at their level of understanding*. Think about how a parent answers a child's questions about where babies come from. We don't tell them everything at once but answer the specific question they ask when they ask it. Don't give children more information than they ask for, are ready to hear, or can process at any one time. Children must always know they are permitted to ask questions, discuss their concerns, and express their feelings. It is prudent for the adults in the immediate surviving family to agree upon what facts will be presented to the children and how, in order to avoid further confusing them with different versions or points of view. A primary adult, perhaps the surviving parent, will answer the child's questions directly, honestly, and as calmly as possible, without going into explicit detail that would cause further anxiety and fear. Weeks, months, even years, after the death, a surviving child may ask for more information and, again, answers should be age appropriate. Be prepared to listen when a child is ready to talk or express his feelings, ideally in an undisturbed setting.

Even a very young child will be aware that something is wrong and that people are very upset. When their questions are dismissed and their need to understand or to be included is neglected, children can easily get the message that it isn't OK to ask questions, and they will be even more confused and frustrated. Young children are not equipped to express or manage their feelings. A surviving child may react to a death and to the changed behavior of the surviving family in ways that add more stress to an already distressed situation. Often a child will express her discomfort and need to be soothed by whining, wanting to be held, quarreling with other children, bedwetting, thumb sucking, or other ways of gaining attention. Of course the adults at this time are in the worst possible emotional position to provide the attention the child needs.

Jenny, a young mother widowed by suicide, instinctively addressed her children's questions and grief needs in a loving and healthy manner and has given permission for the actions she took in the aftermath of her husband's suicide to be shared. When his occasional bouts of depression grew more frequent and intense, Jenny shared her concern with his mother and sister, asking their support in convincing him to get help. As he grew increasingly irritable, had crying spells, and made veiled suicide threats, Jenny was insistent, then adamant that he see a counselor. He reluctantly agreed to make an appointment. But later that week when Jenny and her two sons, Eric, age eight, and Brandon, almost four, came home following an afternoon shopping trip, everything was quiet, too quiet. Jenny was disturbed by an unusual odor. She sent the boys to play in their rooms before she went through the laundry room to open the door to the garage. Strong gaseous fumes assaulted her, and she could see her husband slumped in the front seat of the car. She climbed over some packing boxes to reach him in an attempt to drag him from the car. Unable to revive him, Jenny called 911 and went to get a neighbor to help before returning to the garage. She called for her boys to get out of the house due to the carbon monoxide and looked up to see Eric peeking into the garage. He asked what was wrong with daddy. She quickly moved the boys outside, and a neighbor took them to her home. Efforts of emergency and hospital staff were too late. Jenny's husband was dead.

Hours later when Jenny went from the hospital to her parents' home, where her children had been taken, she found the house full of distressed people. Jenny took her sons into a bedroom, away from the gathering of friends and family, and held them as she told them their daddy had died and that meant he wasn't ever coming back. Eric had overheard the word suicide and asked what it meant. Jenny told them suicide was when a person's brain got sick and caused them to do something on purpose to make him/herself die. She explained that daddy's brain had that sickness and it caused him to make himself die. She assured them that her brain was healthy and so were theirs. She repeatedly reassured Eric and Brandon that daddy had loved them very much and would not have left them if his brain had not been sick. Because Eric did not want to live in their house since "now there are only three of us," Jenny and her sons lived with her parents for eight months until the house was sold.

Jenny's youngest son, Brandon, was concerned about what would happen to him and Eric if Jenny died too. Sensitive to the boy's anxiety issues, Jenny was almost inseparable from them in the first months of their loss, constantly reassuring them that she wasn't going to leave them and that the three of them were still a family. She told them they would all be very sad for a long time but if they talked together about their feelings and about daddy it would help them feel better. Jenny's tears frightened the boys. Although she shared many tears with her sons she shed a great many more in private.

Jenny had enjoyed a close relationship with her husband's family. His sister had been the boys' day-care provider while Jenny and her husband worked. From the time Jenny's husband was pronounced dead at the hospital, his mother and immediate family blamed Jenny for his death. They withdrew all friendliness and support and paid scant attention to her sons. This separation from a nurturing source was an added loss to Eric and Brandon, compounding their anxiety. Rare invitations extended to the boys did not include Jenny. She made excuses to her sons about why they weren't invited to birthday and holiday celebrations and kept them busy, hoping they wouldn't realize they had been left out. Jenny planned frequent interesting, educational, or fun things for the three of them to look forward to so her sons would have the relief of anticipation to distract them from the pain of their father's death.

Within days of her husband's death Jenny sought counseling for herself and her sons. Brandon regressed to infant behavior, crying, speaking in baby talk, wanting a bottle, wetting the bed, and wanting to be held and rocked like a baby. The children's counselor advised Jenny to tend him as if he were still a baby, and within a few weeks Brandon got over his need to be an infant.

From the onset of their bereavement Eric was very angry and would explode over insignificant issues. He began hurting himself by banging his head, rubbing his head on the carpet causing rug burns, and picking at his skin until he made sores. He developed a constant, nervous cough and had choking spells when he became upset. Jenny discussed some of Eric's problems with his teachers, and they cooperated in helping Eric overcome plummeting grades. Over time various therapists and hospital physicians helped Eric work through many of his anxiety issues. Jenny was very cautious in choosing therapists. When a male therapist told Eric that he was now the man of the family Jenny didn't hesitate to dismiss him. "Eric is eight years old, just a little boy," she pointed out, "and he doesn't need the added burden of feeling responsible for his family. I am the mother and Eric needs to know I will take care of him and his brother."

Five years after their father's death, Brandon has regained his easygoing personality, is doing well in school, and is active in sports. Eric has overcome many of the problems that so deeply concerned his mother. He, too, is involved in sports, doing well in school, and his counseling sessions have ceased.

The father of one of Eric's friends died and his mother remarried. The friend told Eric that stepfathers weren't all that great. Eric asked his mother if she was going to get married again. Jenny answered that no one would ever replace their father but she hoped someday there would be another man she could love. She also told him that the three of them were a package deal and if she did remarry it would be to someone they would like very much and who would like them very much in return.

Jenny received her B.A. degree three years after her husband's death. They moved into a new home, and their lives have regained a semblance of order. Jenny and her sons undoubtedly will continue to deal with issues arising from the death of her husband and their father the rest of their lives. They have suffered tremendous loss and pain; they have persevered to overcome nightmarish adversity. And they have made healthy progress and laid a foundation for coping well in the future. Jenny believes that having survived the past five years, they can survive anything.

Appropriately addressing needs of children bereaved by suicide is very important to their future mental health. As difficult as it is to acknowledge, the deceased individual has modeled to the surviving child how one can deal with pain and problems. The negative role modeling must be refuted in the ways the child's grief is addressed. Jenny repeatedly reassured her sons, "Daddy's brain was sick. His sick brain caused him to end his life. My brain is fine, so is yours." This relieved anxiety about themselves and their remaining family. Hopefully, Jenny also told her sons that sick brains can get better or well with the help of a good "brain doctor" should they know of someone with a sick brain in the future.

ഇ)രു

Sam shot and injured his girlfriend before killing himself the day after his half-brother's fourth birthday. Sam's half-siblings, Faith, six, and Abe, four, were too young to grasp the concept of death as permanent and expected their brother to come back. At almost twelve, Abe experiences a sense of loss for his brother but grieves deeply for having few memories of him. As Abe neared his eleventh birthday he asked his parents what he had done wrong on his fourth birthday that made his brother kill himself. His question reminded his parents that at milestones throughout their surviving children's lives they will need to process grief for their brother's death. Faith, now fourteen, is still angry because she and Abe were not allowed to sit at the front of the church with her parents at Sam's funeral, reminding us of the importance of inclusion and uniting the family to grieve. Faith had to turn aside hateful barbs when a classmate told her Sam was in hell because he tried to kill someone.

Protecting the child's future begins in the immediate aftermath of the death when she needs/wants to know what has happened. Care should be taken not to glorify the person or how they died. To do so could send the message that suicide is acceptable, even exceptional or honorable. On the other hand, the family must take care not to condemn the deceased or allow any references to their being evil, worthless, or cowardly. To do so affects the child's own self-image; she may assume that she, too, is an evil or worthless coward doomed to follow suit.

The surviving child should not be unfavorably compared with the deceased by angry statements such as, "You act just like your father!" This might cause the child to believe that, because he is like his deceased father he is destined, even obliged, to take the same action. A surviving child must be reinforced with positive comments such as, "You remind me of your mother when you smile"; "Your daddy could draw wonderful pictures, just as you do"; "Let's use your mother's cookie recipe. She was such a good cook"; "Your dad loved to read. He would be so glad that you do, too."

Laying a foundation for the future well-being of a child be-reaved by suicide takes great patience at a time when other immediate survivors are struggling with their own acute grief. Support from the entire surviving family unit, learning how to offer positive reinforcement, and providing counseling with therapists who understand the needs of grieving children and the complexities of suicide bereavement—all these are vital. Caregivers must help guide the surviving children to grieve in a healthy manner, enabling them to enjoy a stable and happy future.

At some time during the surviving child's adolescent or adult life he/she will ask for and should be given facts about the death as they are known. Each time a child asks and receives new information he/she will need to assimilate and process that in-formation, sometimes in a manner much like a grief response. At every stage in the child's life throughout their life, he/she will revisit the loss of their parent and will need to readjust the present to the past. The readjustment is often expressed as regret, "I wish my mother could have seen me in my prom dress." "My father should have been here to walk me down the aisle." "My dad would have been so proud of me graduating at the top of my class." This may happen when the child gradu-ates from high school or college, when she marries, when she has children of her own, or at a time of another loss within the family—anytime there is a significant event in that surviving child's life.

A few support groups for children grieving a suicide have been formed, some in conjunction with adult suicide bereave-ment groups, some autonomous. Children are age-grouped and address grief through art, journaling, play, relaxation, coping techniques, and sharing. Groups are either ongoing or time-limited to six or eight weeks and operate under the direction of a professional with expertise in child development and knowl-edge of suicide and suicide bereavement. Reports from these groups are sparse but positive. One group director reports a significant rise in a teenage boy's grades after several weeks attendance. A girl surviving her father's suicide had been suicidal herself before participating in a group specific to suicide loss. A teenager with an eating disorder following a family member's suicide was referred for therapy by an alert group staff.

It is not surprising that a bereaved child needs the same reinforcement and validation that adults bereaved by suicide need: I am not the only one. I am not alone.

Grandparent Grief

"...Bone of my bone, and flesh of my flesh..."

Genesis 2:23

My parents were guests in our home the night my son ended his life. My father had been the last to talk with him as they sat visiting after the rest of us retired. My father and my son shared a close relationship. Dad was the first to wonder why he hadn't known. Was there something Kent said that he had missed? Kent had talked to my father at length about his new job and the invitation to speak the following day at a sales meeting. Kent hadn't seemed anxious or mentioned that anything was bothering him. I saw my mother, seemingly the source of unlimited strength and faith, crumple and age before my eyes. My parents and my husband's widowed mother made no judgment, nor did they ask for or expect attention or support. They stayed on the periphery of the family grieving circle, welcoming callers, listing gifts of flowers, food, and phone calls, expressing concern for my husband and myself, looking for ways to tend and comfort us. They spoke little of their own feelings in the days following Kent's death. I felt great compassion for the pain they experienced from the death of this beloved grandson but I did not have the wits or energy to express it.

For months after my parents returned to their home in another state, my mother called me every day (this was before "unlimited free minutes"). Most calls were brief. She would ask about our well-being, share any news, and tell me she loved me. Sometimes it was a long conversation as I needed to say the same things, ask the same questions of myself, rehearsing my own motherhood over and over again to find the part I might have played in his despair. I desperately needed and received my parents' reassurance of my own good parenting. I don't recall ever asking any of my son's grandparents how they were doing. My obsession with my own grief and loss blinded me to theirs.

About three years after my son's death, my parents attended the suicide bereavement support group my husband and I had founded. Coincidentally, the same evening another pair of newly bereaved grandparents attended. A good portion of the group discussion focused upon the loss and grief of grandparents. All four spoke of the anguish of losing their grandchild, in both cases a grandson. Each became very emotional when they spoke of the pain of seeing their own child suffer and the helplessness of knowing there was nothing they could do to assuage their child's anguish.

Insights gained from talking with grandparents who survive the suicide of a grandchild have showed me that grandparents grieve on two dimensions. They grieve their loss of a grandchild, often a grandchild they cuddled, tended, and loved since he/she was a baby. They suffer as well for the anguish of their own child, all the while knowing there is no balm, no kiss, no distraction that can ease the pain their child has suffered. Their grief may be magnified by judgment about suicide that prevailed from their youth. For some grandparents, the death of a child of their own years earlier makes things even harder as they revisit that earlier bereavement and their firsthand knowledge of the agony resulting from the death of one's child.

There are situations that cause the surviving grandparent to become the guardian of a deceased child's child. Bonnie was such a grandmother. Her daughter had a son out of wedlock and made her home with Bonnie. After her daughter ended her life Bonnie was granted guardianship of her three-year-old grandson and, as a single grandparent on Social Security, assumed the responsibility of raising him.

Sometimes the grandparents of young surviving children are separated and alienated from their grandchildren due to circumstances surrounding the death and/or the decision of a surviving spouse. After Edie's forty-year-old son, her only living child,[1] ended his life, his wife, the mother of Edie's only two grandchildren, determined the children would be harmed by a continued relationship with Edie and her husband and would not allow Edie contact with her grandchildren. Edie tried to be understanding. She knew her son's wife was uncomfortable with Edie's deafness and inability to speak distinctly. Edie sent birthday and Christmas cards with checks every year, receiving no response. When the youngest grandchild graduated from high school, he sent Edie an invitation and she eagerly traveled the hundred and fifty miles to attend. But the years of distance had taken their toll. The brief meeting was strained and did not result in the reconciliation or renewed relationship Edie had hoped for.

Many surviving parents have suffered the additional loss of a relationship with their surviving grandchildren. In pursuit of grandparent rights the primary concern must be whether a grandparent's involvement with the grandchild is in the best interest of the surviving grandchild. Grandparents who have enjoyed a deep, loving relationship with a grandchild are more compelled to seek continuation of that relationship after the grandchild's parent (their own child) has died. When circumstances prior to or surrounding the death have caused estrangement from the surviving parent (the daughter-or son-in-law) the surviving grandparents may find themselves without any legal rights for maintaining contact with the grandchild.

---

[1] *Edie's son suffered survivor guilt from the time he was twelve when his father and his two younger siblings were killed in an accident while he was at scout camp. The losses Edie endured in her younger life were compounded by her son's suicide and her alienation from his surviving children. Edie and her second husband invested time and love in the local suicide survivor movement, extending comfort and encouragement to newly bereaved. Edie died at age seventy-two in 2005 without reconciliation with her grandchildren.*

Grandparents can request a mediation session with the surviving parent to find a common meeting ground. The party seeking mediation hires a neutral third party to help the grandparents and the surviving parent create a legally binding agreement that everyone can respect and live with. Grandparents facing resistance to contact with their grandchild may pursue information regarding their state's current laws by researching the state statutes addressing grandparent rights on the Internet or consult an attorney in the field of family law. A bitter fact: there are grandparents who are allowed no further contact with their grandchildren following their own child's death.

Survivors of Military Suicide

"Our friend died on his own battlefield. He was killed in action fighting a civil war. He fought against adversaries that were as real to him as his casket is real to us. They were powerful adversaries. They took toll of his energies and endurance. They exhausted the last vestiges of his courage and strength. At last these adversaries overwhelmed him."

Rev. Warren Stevens

Among the saddest of all deaths by suicide are those that occur among active and former members of the military. Too many courageous men and women have risked their lives again and again and survived bombs and bullets, only to die by their own hand. Some have ended their lives on foreign soil, offering no opportunity for family intervention; others have returned home to the vast relief of their families—and then the family loses them to suicide. *Time Magazine* [1] reports that from the invasion of Afghanistan to April, 2010, 761 American military died in combat. In the same period 817 military ended their life. The grief and frustration of the families surviving these deaths by suicide are unfathomable.

After being deployed three times, twice to Iraq, once to Afghanistan, Paul and Angie's son, Rick, returned to his assigned post and resumed a regular routine. One morning, ready for work, he left the apartment he shared with his girlfriend, opened the trunk of his car, threw in his backpack, picked up a gun that he stored there, and shot himself in the head. There were no apparent signs of depression, no warning. There had been no quarrel with his girlfriend or parents and no problems

---

[1] *Mark Thompson, "Is The U.S. Army Losing Its War on Suicide?" April 13, 2010.*

at work. Paul and Angie struggled to understand why, having escaped death during three combat tours, their only child would deliberately end his own life.

Following his third tour Rick had talked with his father about his guilt at being the sole survivor when the vehicle carrying him and several of his buddies was hit by explosives. Rick had been blown free but landed on his head, suffering a traumatic brain injury (TBI).Paul and Angie recalled that during each deployment Rick had suffered a concussion from explosions.

In pursuit of understanding their son's suicide, Paul and Angie began researching the effects of traumatic brain injury and learned that TBI can lead to a variety of symptoms and disabilities, including emotional and behavioral effects. Cognitive and emotional symptoms include personality and mood change, confusion, trouble with memory, concentration, problems with reasoning, depression, anxiety, and other mental health issues. Paul and Angie do not disregard the probability that Rick also may have suffered Posttraumatic Stress Disorder (PTSD).

The grief resulting from their son's suicide was compounded by a very harsh remark made at the public presentation of a scholarship Paul and Angie awarded a high school ROTC student in Rick's memory. Their son's service to his country was discounted and his honor questioned when the ROTC award presenter referred to the cause of Rick's death as "disgusting." The derogatory remark was publicly repeated several times, at least once in the presence of Paul and Angie. They requested and were permitted the opportunity to confront the ROTC instructor, in the presence of his employer, regarding the statement he made. They received a private apology from him.

Angie felt she was unable to effectively perform her job in a bank and took an indefinite leave of absence. She and Paul became involved with other Gold Star parents in preparing and furnishing the Fallen Hero center on their local military post. They attend a community suicide survivor support group, a newly formed survivor group on post, and local TAPS (Tragedy Assistance Program for Survivors) events. Paul and Angie are making a valiant effort to move on with their lives as they continue to struggle with the heartbreaking loss of their only child, the futility of his death, and the judgment directed toward him.

ΣΟΟΒ

The stress of war is not a factor in all military suicides. For some, it is the stress of preparing to go to war. An avid outdoorsman and expert marksman, Nolan Stites expected to become an exemplary soldier and enlisted in the army reserves' delayed entry program as a high school senior. In early July 2000, he left his Colorado home for basic training at Fort Leonard Wood, Mo.

Upon arrival at Fort Leonard Wood, Pvt. Stites learned Basic Combat Training had been delayed by one week. This delay would prevent him from graduating from basic training in time to participate in Advanced Individual Training he was scheduled for at Sheppard Air Force Base.

Acclimation to Missouri's heat and humidity from Colorado's dry, cool, high-altitude climate was complicated when Nolan severely sunburned his head. Soon thereafter he began having trouble thinking clearly, following orders, reading, and writing. During a phone call to his father, Nolan sounded anxious and panicky. He said he was really "messing up." He had developed shin splints and couldn't eat or sleep. He was unable to do more than three push-ups although he could easily do fifty before he left home. In a second call to his parents, Nolan said he had never been so depressed in all his life because he was one of the worst two soldiers in his platoon and was holding the platoon back.

Nolan developed bladder problems and wet himself during an exercise. After two more wetting incidents, Nolan told a buddy he wished he could die. The buddy went with him to see the chaplain. Nolan told the chaplain he was depressed and had suicidal thoughts. This was immediately reported to the company commander, who placed Nolan on full unit watch[2], removed him from all training, and ordered him to relinquish his belt and bootlaces. He was ordered to move his mattress into the war room, where he was to sleep under guard by peers. He was ostracized as a team member and accused of faking mental problems. Witnesses reported that during formation a drill sergeant belittled Nolan in front of his platoon, saying they would be better off without him and that he should kill himself.

Nolan's physical examination did not indicate any illness other than constipation due to not drinking enough water. His only appointment with a mental health provider took place after five days on unit suicide watch, with the social worker determining that, although Nolan was depressed and expressed a sense of doom, he was not suicidal. The mental health evaluation stated Nolan might have a learning disability, was not suitable for service, and should not be given weapons due to his level of anxiety. He recommended Nolan remain on full unit watch with follow up the next week and be given an Entry Level Separation from the service. Nolan's dream of becoming a soldier was over.

Nolan was moved back to his third floor room where he remained on unit suicide watch for ten more days. Two days before he died, Nolan wrote his drill sergeant a note begging for help and apologizing for any trouble he had caused his platoon. No doctor ever saw the note. Nolan called his parents telling them he wasn't doing well and didn't know if he could make it until his birthday. His father contacted the Red Cross to intervene. A Red Cross contact talked with Nolan and responded to his father regarding their deep concern. Nolan's drill sergeant was advised.

Sometime shortly before he died Nolan wrote a letter to his parents thanking them for their love and told them he "didn't know how to get help," that "he had failed," and "God could never forgive him for disgracing his country and family." Two days before his nineteenth birthday, during a guard shift exchange, Nolan ended fifteen days of unit watch when he removed the screen from his window, climbed out onto the ledge, and stepped off above a concrete stairwell three stories below.

Nolan's father, Richard, believes his son's death directly resulted from the humiliation of unit watch. Richard spent over ten years collecting information, writing letters to lawmakers protesting unit watch, and advocating against its use. In April 2010 Richard received a copy of a Department of Defense report sent to all military installations recommending the discontinuance of unit watch except for emergency situations. For the first time in ten years Richard slept through the night.

Nolan's father and mother honor Nolan's memory by being TAPS peer mentors to military parents grieving suicide and facilitate a suicide bereavement support group for military survivors at Fort Carson, Colo.

℘℘℘

"Suicide seems to wipe out the life lived and replace it with how that person dies," says Kim. "When my husband, John, ended his life, it was as if he went from Hero to Zero in an instant." Kim fears her husband will be remembered for how he died rather than how he lived.

---

[2] *FULL UNIT WATCH This approach is used when a soldier has some potential to act out in his unit or when a soldier refused to contract with their Unit or Consultant not to injure themselves. 1. The Drill Sergeant (DS) removes all medications or other potential items that could be used to gesture or attempt suicide... shoe strings, belt, etc. 2. The Soldier is required to move to the CQ area at night to sleep under the supervision of the CQ. The Soldier may or may not be working with the platoon depending on the situation. 3. The Soldier will shave under supervision of the DS or their designee. 4. Community Mental Health Services (CMHS) continues to monitor the soldier and consult with the Soldier's unit in order to alter or change the level of the watch. 5. The Soldier often remains in training under full unit watch but in some cases the solder may be in RFT status and under supervision of the Orderly Room personnel. 6. The Soldier will be under observation at all times.*

John, a decorated Cobra gunship pilot, lived life to the fullest. He was funny, loyal, loving, dedicated, and revered by the Marines he led. John had battled depression over the years, but as a pilot in the Marine Corps, he believed getting help or telling anyone would end his career. He had overcome previous depressive episodes by physically pushing his way through them and "waiting it out." John saw his bouts of depression as weak and ridiculous. He was worried that people would find out and repeatedly made Kim promise to keep it a secret. John was ashamed he had put Kim through his bouts of depression and vowed, "I will never do that to you again." Kim, a social worker, desperately wanted John to get help but feared telling anyone would betray him and maybe make things worse.

In their Massachusetts home, on February 6, 2005, Kim and her two sons, Joey, ten, and Billy, eight, watched the family's favorite team, the Patriots, win the Super Bowl. The boys couldn't wait to share their excitement with their father, who was temporarily staying in a hotel in Carlsbad, California. When he didn't answer their calls Kim assumed he was at a Super Bowl party and couldn't hear the ring. Alarms went off in Kim's head when he finally answered and told her he had been in his room but hadn't watched the game. She knew he was battling another bout of depression but she had not known it had reached such a dangerous level. Kim calmly told him, "John, if you are feeling so bad that you couldn't watch the game, you have to get help. I don't care if you never fly again, or if you have to leave the Marine Corps. We will be okay. You have to get help." He was quiet for a moment and said "I know I have to, but this is going to be the end of everything. I am supposed to go back to Iraq in March. They will think I just don't want to go, that I am making it up. They will never let me lead again. They are depending on me to lead these young guys. I will let everyone down."

Kim could hear the desperation in his voice and asked, "Are you feeling so bad that you could hurt yourself? Or kill yourself?" Kim was greatly relieved when John replied, "I could never do that to you and the boys." She told him to go to the clinic on base and tell them how bad his depression was. She asked him to call her when he got there and asked if he wanted her to call someone to take him, to which he quickly responded "NO! I don't want anyone to see me like this. I can drive myself, but I might not be able to call you because there is not good reception on base." Kim told John she loved him and that they could get through this.

Despite the fact John was to fly home on Thursday to celebrate Joey's eleventh birthday, Kim immediately booked a red-eye flight to California. She knew admitting to the Marine Corps that he was depressed was the most difficult thing John would ever do.

Upon arriving at the San Diego airport early the next morning, Kim received no answer when she called John's number. She called both the hospital emergency room and the outpatient clinic and asked if Major John Ruocco had checked in. He had not. She called his office and learned he hadn't shown up for work. She remembers her numbness and thinking, "I am too late."

Kim rented a car and drove toward Carlsbad, watching for a Ramada Inn. As she parked her car she saw a car with Marine stickers parked haphazardly. The man behind the motel desk was on the phone, frantically saying, "What do I do? I have never had this happen." Kim knew he was talking about John and said, "It's my husband! Where is he? Can you take me to him?" The man looked at her, panic on his face, slowly backed into another room, and closed the door. Kim started yelling, "Does anyone know where my husband is? Can anyone take me to my husband?" A kindly Hispanic woman took her hand and led Kim to the third floor. As she rounded the corner a Marine was coming out of a room, crying. Kim fell to the ground, screaming. She knew.

A detective asked Kim a million questions "Do you have money problems, marital problems? Was he having an affair?" She could only think of one thing. How was she going to tell her boys? How does one tell eight and ten year olds that their dad, their hero who made it home safely from a war zone, has taken his own life? When a trauma specialist arrived, Kim asked her, "What do I tell my children? How do I tell my children?" Kim was told, "They are too young to understand the concept of suicide. You should tell them that it was an accident." A priest arrived. Kim asked him, "What should I tell my children?" He looked at her for what seemed like forever and replied, "You know what the Church believes about suicide." "No, I don't," she said. He finally said, "That it is a sin." Kim was enraged and yelled at him, "Are you telling me that I am supposed to tell my children that their Dad is not only dead but he is in hell? Is that what you are telling me?" He just looked at her. Kim was handed a phone with her brother-in-law on the line. She told him to tell the children that John had died in an accident.

Kim was in panic on the plane ride home. She had told her children the biggest lie of their lives. She would have to be careful not to let them find out. She could not bring them to their church for fear of what they would be told. She would have to make sure every adult knew not to say anything to them. She worried that they would overhear someone talking about it or they would read something. What if other children found out the truth and told them? Or worse, what if other kids found out the truth and used it to bully them? After the reaction of the hotel staff, Kim worried about how people would respond to her. Would they blame her? Would they be angry at her? Would they turn their back on her and run away as if this terrible thing was contagious?

During John's funeral a peer said, "John was the dad everyone should be, the husband our wives all wanted us to be, and the Marine we all aspired to be." They were always the couple, the family that people admired. Would people think it was all a lie? Did Kim think it was a lie? Her world was turned upside down. Things she knew to be true were no longer so. If she could miss this, how could she trust her instincts about anything else? She was overcome with guilt. "Why didn't I call 911? Why didn't I send a friend to the room? Why didn't I get help for him sooner? It is my fault. I have a master's degree in social work. I have helped many people overcome depression and avoid suicide. Why did I not save the person I loved the most? Looking back it seems so clear. I saw the blank look in his eyes. I heard the desperation in his voice. I felt his pain. Why didn't I do more?"

Six years after the death of her husband, Kim has learned a lot about herself, her family, and suicide. She now knows enough about her husband's death to say, "It is what it is. If I knew then what I know now, I might have done things differently. "Kim shares that when her husband died, her life as she had known it died too, as if it had burned to the ground and she had to start from scratch. Her minister, Reverend Laura Biddle, compared this to the story of the phoenix. Kim could rebuild her family in any way she chose; she had an opportunity to become stronger and, in some ways, better than ever.

Kim started with her children, telling them the truth about how their dad died. She reassured them that it was not their fault. She told them that he was sick and didn't get help for it. She promised them that from that day forward she would tell them the truth, that they could ask her anything and she would try to answer it. She assured them that she would take care of herself and both of them and they would get through this together.

Kim believes that when people are so sick as to take their own life, God knows and wraps His loving arms around them. She has shared this belief with religious leaders in her community and most agree. She believes love doesn't die, that her relationship with John continues. She talks to John, asking for his guidance and strength and believes it comes to her. She believes that "You can't prevent what you can't predict"; had she thought John would actually kill himself, she would have responded differently. Kim strongly believes that God has a plan that she doesn't understand. She prays that it will be revealed to her and that she can fulfill it.

Kim Ruocco currently manages the TAPS suicide outreach and education programs, providing suicide postvention (aftermath support) and prevention services and seminars around the country. (Edwin Shneidman coined the word *postvention* and defined it as suicide prevention for the next generations.)

Prior to July 2011, families of military suicide did not receive condolence letters from the U.S. president, unlike surviving families of other causes of death. On July 5, 2011, the White House announced that families of military who end their life in combat zones will receive condolence letters from the president just like families of troops that die in other ways. This action is not retroactive nor does it include stateside military suicides.

PRACTICAL PIECES

Assuming or Assigning Blame

"The blame is his who chooses: God is blameless."

Plato, *The Republic*

When someone we love dies, our first anguished cry is how? How did the death occur? When someone we love ends their life, our first anguished cry is why? Why did the suicide come to be? What was so bad as to cause this beloved person to end their life? Was he/she in such pain that death was the only way of finding peace? What part did others play in this tragedy?

Bereaved significant others are often reluctant to assign the deceased responsibility for the act. We want someone to step up to the plate and accept responsibility. It may be the surviving spouse that the deceased's family of origin blames, singling out separation or the inability to be a good marriage partner, remembering lack of support, arguments that may have occurred in the marriage, inability to promote the deceased spouse's self-confidence. Or it may be the surviving spouse who lays the blame upon the family of origin with criticisms of how the victim was raised, perhaps citing abuse or neglect. It may be one parent blaming the other, especially in the case of a youth whose parents are separated or divorced; "you were too strict,"; "you were too lenient", "you were never around,"; "you always criticized." The blame list is endless.

Too frequently the surviving parents of an adult child fix the blame for the suicide upon their child's spouse, compounding the grief of the surviving husband or wife. Blaming the spouse deprives all parties of uniting in their bereavement, complicates the grieving process with conflict and magnified anger, and is very destructive to surviving children. Irreversible damage can be done to surviving relationships before the parent survivor accepts the fact that no marriage partner has the power to cause the other to deliberately end his/her life. Even though the marriage may have been unhappy, even toxic and abusive, there are ways of dissolving a relationship other than ending one's own life.

Playing the blame game is destructive and unproductive. Knowing the reason or the cause of our loved one's suicide changes nothing. Blaming another individual or assuming responsibility ourselves offers no comfort nor does it end our grief, but it lays a tremendous added burden of conflict and endangered relationships.

The wish to somehow vindicate the decedent's action is futile. To achieve healthy healing it is necessary to put aside thoughts of another's blame, responsibility and desire for retribution or redemption. Retribution and redemption are unachievable.

Difficult though it is, we must allow responsibility for the death to rest with the one who completed the act. Our husband, our sibling, our parent, our child . . . our dead loved one is the person responsible. It is their pain and they way they resolved it that causes our loss and grief. Regardless of circumstance or what we or someone else did or failed to do that we believe contributed to their pain, the final decision was theirs. For another to be assigned or to assume responsibility for that decision diminishes our loved one's personhood, minimizes the magnitude of their pain, and negates the tremendous effort they invested in trying to live.

Closure and Recovery

"People are forever changed by the experience of grief in their lives. We, as humans, do not 'get over' our grief, but work to reconcile ourselves to it."

Alan Wolfelt, PhD, *The Journey Through Grief*

Reporters, clergy, mental health professionals, even grief counselors speak often of the need for closure following a death; some speak of grief recovery. They suggest that one must have closure in order to move through the rest of one's life in a healthy, stable manner. A recent news update on a missing child reported that her body had been found and identified. The reporter mused that now the parents could have closure. While this child's parents no longer fear what their child is enduring, they also no longer hope that she lives. Perhaps closure means that now that they know she is dead they can grieve her death and, at some point, recover from that grief.

What is closure and what has to happen for a bereaved person to achieve it? The dictionary defines closure as the act of shutting; a closed condition or the end; the finish; the conclusion. Does this mean that grief is eventually finished, that there is an end to yearning, to feeling adrift, overwhelmed with pain and fearful of the future without the loved one? Does closure mean the bereaved no longer weeps and rages, feels emptiness, sadness, longing or heartache? Has the mourner reached a time when obsession with the loss, "if only" and "what might have been" no longer matter, are over, finished, "closed"? Does closure mean mourning has been completed?

Exchanges with other suicide bereaved cause me to question whether there is such a thing as closure after the death of someone dearly loved, especially when suicide is the cause of death. Certainly closure is not an instant transformation from the agony of loss to acceptance, understanding, and revived sense of well-being and happiness. Perhaps *closure* is a vague, indefinable term for moving from acute grief to less intense strata of mourning. Perhaps the definition of the term includes the mourner's acknowledgment of the fact of death, even reconciliation to the cause of the death being suicide. Perhaps it involves the suicide bereaved eventually moving productively through their lives, forever without answers to their myriad of questions. Perhaps closure has different meaning for different mourners.

And then there is *recovery*, a word defined as getting back what has been lost or taken away, or being restored to good health following an illness. Is there recovery after the death of a loved one? Are grievers restored to their former state? In the first days of our grief we may pray that what has happened is a very bad dream and that we will awaken and have recovered our loved one, have our old life back, and go back to "normal." But even in our most desperate yearning we can intellectualize the futility of that dream of recovering the dead. We know that our old life, the one we lived before our loved one died, is gone. We begin to understand that a new normal has begun to unfold.

Dear mourner, if you cannot identify a time when your "grief case" closed, a time when the pain of your loss ended, a time when you have "recovered" from your grief, do not be concerned.You are in good company. I doubt very few mourners can pinpoint a time of closure or recovery.

Mourning is a life's work in progress. While there is no end to emotional response to the death of someone dear, there is growth, change, and healing. Acute grief does not last forever. Our inconsolable anguish gentles into sorrow that is tolerable. Our sense of guilt or unmet responsibility is redefined as regret. Our anger is relinquished to be replaced by knowledge, understanding, and forgiveness. Our feelings of despair and helplessness are slowly replaced with hope and renewed confidence. Our wound becomes less and less tender and vulnerable to injury from stigma and insensitive remarks. We again glimpse the joy of being alive. We are hopeful. Though we never recover what has been lost or the life we enjoyed before the death occurred, we do see a future beyond merely surviving . . . a future that holds the promise of good times, good living, and the blessing of memories of that lost love. There comes a time when we recognize and appreciate that part of who we are, and who we will become, is the life we shared with them.

Deeds of Omission and Commission

"Call ignorance my sorrow, not my sin."

Robert Browning, *The Ring and the Book*

Many who survive a loved one's suicide were aware of the loved one's mental illness and did everything in their power to help the individual cope with, control, or overcome the illness. Others were very aware that their loved one suffered an addictive disorder and did their utmost be informed and supportive. Yet, despite all that support and vigilance, the loved one ended his or her life. Survivors may be strengthened and comforted in the knowledge that they did all they possibly could have done. But it is not unusual, even in these cases, for the survivor to believe there must have been something left undone that would have saved the life, or that something they said or did contributed to their loved one's death.

Many who survive a suicide had no knowledge that mental illness was the basis of the confusion, agitation, irritation, and irrational behavior exhibited by their loved one. The deceased family member may have been very adept at hiding thoughts of suicide. Often these survivors live with a tremendous burden of the *If only's*. "If only I had known," "If only I had called," "If only I had been more patient." They believe that they could have said something or taken some action that would have changed what now can never be changed.

Lynne, Chris's wife and the mother of his three-month-old daughter, had suffered mental illness most of her life. There would be times when she appeared very well; then, quite suddenly, she would fall into deep depression. Chris believes he may never have known his wife when she wasn't mentally ill. Three months following the birth of their daughter, believing Lynne was suicidal during an especially severe bout of depression, Chris took her to a mental hospital for the third time in a week, asking that she not be released until she was stable. At work the following day Chris received a call from Lynne telling him she had been released from the hospital and was in a cab on her way home. Chris immediately left work to drive home. Heavy traffic delayed him. He arrived to find the door to their apartment open. Lynne's car had not been moved from the parking lot but Lynne could not be found. During his frantic search a neighbor approached him and inquired about Lynne. She told Chris his wife had fallen from their sixth-floor balcony and an ambulance had taken her to the hospital. The third hospital Chris called advised him she was being treated in the emergency room. Lynne died from her injuries several hours later. Even though Chris knew he had done the best that he could to keep Lynne safe, he flogged himself with recrimination for not having taken her to a different hospital, for not foreseeing the hospital might release her, for not having known she was terminally ill even though doctors determined otherwise.

Chris worked through his grief within a support group. As a single parent, Chris focuses on the well-being of his daughter, now twelve. Occasionally he speaks on a conference panel about Lynne and her struggle with mental illness.

෨෬

According to the American Foundation of Suicide Prevention, 7 percent of persons with alcohol dependency will end their lives and alcohol is a factor in 30 percent of all suicides. Most families of alcoholics are unaware of these facts or unprepared to react appropriately even when they are.

Ron was accustomed to relaxing every evening by drinking a couple of beers. Ron's father had been recovering alcoholic, active in Alcoholics Anonymous. Ron's oldest son, David, had a drinking problem. Ron talked with David frequently about his drinking, urging him to attend AA or check himself into a rehabilitation facility. Upon contacting a Denver rehab hospital, Ron and his wife were told that David would not be admitted into their program unless he was drunk at the time of intake. Uncomfortable with this approach, they did not investigate other rehab facilities.

When David was in his late twenties, his wife of two years divorced him, leaving him deeply in debt. To protect David from bankruptcy, his parents loaned him money and invited David to make his home with them until he could get back on his feet. David moved into his parents' home promising to keep appointments with his addiction counselor, attend AA meetings, and work hard to attain consistent sobriety. David and Ron signed an agreement written by Ron, stating that if David fell off the wagon he would be expected to vacate his parents' home.

At thirty years of age David was ashamed of having to live with his parents. Although he was doing very well at a good job and attending AA meetings, he suffered several backslides by drinking on weekends. Each time Ron would discuss their agreement and David's need to gain control of his drinking. Ron would overrule his own "tough love" edict and give an apologetic David another chance. During the months with his parents, David was able to pay back the loan and save for a down payment on a condo, finalizing the purchase in late January.

On a January afternoon, after Ron had returned home from an overnight trip, he sat drinking a beer as he watched a football game when David came up the stairs from his bedroom. David was hung over. It was the last straw. Ron told David, "I've had it. You're out of here."David replied that he had no place to go and asked if he could he stay two more weeks until he could move into his condo. Ron told him no, he had used up all his second chances, and he could stay with some of his friends. Ron went to David's room and began carrying drawers full of David's belongings outside, piling them in the yard.

Sometime after Ron had finished moving David's possessions outside, David was found lying in the snow, dead from a self-inflicted gunshot wound.

Nearly out of his mind with remorse, Ron assumed absolute responsibility for David's death. He repeatedly reviewed his actions of that day. Why had he chosen that particular moment to exercise tough love? Why hadn't he sat down with David one more time to discuss the situation rationally? What did two weeks matter? Ron repeatedly chastised himself; knowing that even a couple of beers altered his thinking, why had he had allowed himself to react in a knee-jerk fashion?

Ron visited an addiction counselor a few times and was assured that David was responsible for David's death, but Ron held fast to the belief that the responsibility was his alone. He attended a suicide bereavement support group, where he found some comfort knowing he wasn't the only parent who felt responsible following the suicide of their child. When another group participant needed help moving, Ron was the first to volunteer. He donated generously when a survivor needed help with utility payment. He always responded to the need of another parent with a similar situation by sharing and offering encouragement. Not uncommonly, Ron's opening statement was, "I killed my son as surely as if I had held the gun."

For four years Ron clung to his perceived guilt, bringing it out every day to remind himself of his failure as a father. His sense of guilt prevented him from mourning with David's mother and siblings. The burden of guilt he carried impeded his own healing, for he constantly reminded himself that because of him his son was dead; because of him the family had suffered a devastating loss.

Then Ron discovered Model T Fords. He saw them, learned about them, bought one, then another, began investing his thought and energy in restoring them. He and another Model T enthusiast traveled across three states at twenty-five miles per hour to attend a rally, and Ron loved every minute of it. This trip may have been Ron's first peaceful period in a very long time.

Ron has begun to understand that he has given his feelings of guilt power over future happiness with his family. He is making a great effort to forgive himself for doing what he thought was the right thing at the time. He is learning to rethink his role in David's death, replacing the word guilt with the word regret, and he recognizes how changing that word lifts a huge burden from his heart. Ron is now able to say, "I deeply regret I chose that time to draw a line in the sand." A statement made by Ron echoes the thoughts of all parents who confronted or chastised their child before that child ended their life, "For the rest of my life I will profoundly regret that my last words to him were the last straw for him."

There are those who survive after a death by suicide where no mental illness has been diagnosed or where none is present, where drinking or addiction was not a factor, where the death was seemingly a spontaneous or impetuous act, perhaps following an adverse situation or environmental influence. These family members, too, suffer the burden of feeling responsible, that they did or said something that tipped the balance or that they should somehow have foreseen the possibility of suicide. This is especially true for the survivor who was in conflict with their deceased family member prior to the suicide.

Seventeen years old, Evan, a top student, talented athlete, popular with his peers, and the pride of his family, was arrested for shoplifting and released to the custody of his parents. Evan had more than enough money in his pocket to pay for the item. Richard, Evan's father, severely chastised Evan, told him he had shamed the entire family, and restricted him to school and church activities until the end of the year. The next day Evan shot himself to death. Richard believes his chastisement caused Evan to end his life. Richard found little consolation in reassurance that he had done what most conscientious fathers would have done.

Deeds of omission and commission place a tremendous overload on the shoulders of suicide bereaved. *If only* is a common statement from suicide bereaved, for each one wants to turn back the clock, to change history, to have do-overs. A survivor's sense of omnipotence often causes him to believe he could have stopped the loved one's final act if only they had had a last opportunity to talk, *if only* he had responded in a different manner.

What suicide bereaved often fail to consider is the length of time their loved one may have continued to live *because* of them, because of the encouragement, love, praise, and reinforcement they extended. There is no way to know the duration of that extension. It may only have been an hour or a day, maybe a week or a month. But it was an hour, day, week, or month the loved one would not have lived otherwise.

There is a great difference between *feeling* a sense of unmet responsibility after a suicide and *being* responsible for the act. *Feeling* responsible is the struggle with one's omnipotence. It is not unusual for someone close to the individual who has ended his/her life to believe, consciously or unconsciously, "My strength, my love, my power, my presence, my words or my action could have kept them alive." This mind set implies "I am all-powerful"; "I have the power to control and to protect." One may even believe, "Had I been in charge, had I been responsible, this death would not have occurred." The bottom line: you were not in charge and you are not responsible.

Assuming responsibility for their child's act is a common reaction of parents surviving a youth's suicide. They are reluctant to relinquish control over their child's life . . . and death. How very difficult it is to allow a beloved child this degree of control over his/her life, and yours! Yet eventually it is necessary to allow the responsibility for the death to rest with the one who caused the death, even one so young.

To Move or Not to Move

"Don't try to destroy a beautiful part of your life because remembering it hurts. As children of today and tomorrow, we are also children of yesterday. The past still travels with us and what has been, makes us what we are."

Rabbi Earl Grollman, *Living When A Loved One Has Died*

When the death, or the injury that ended in death, occurs in the home, it is not uncommon for the family to consider moving to a new residence. Surviving family members often want to leave the place their loved one ended their life. The survivor who finds the body may feel what he or she viewed makes it impossible to continue to live in the house. The wish to separate oneself from the site of the tragedy is understandable. When the residence is a rented house or apartment, the decision to move is not too difficult. But when the residence is a long-time family home, the decision can be viewed as another loss, very stressful and heart wrenching.

My son shot himself in the family room of the home we had built fourteen years before. Would we ever again be able to sit in front of the family room fireplace? I knew exactly where he lay when we found him. Would it be possible ever to look at that area of the room without recalling terrible images? Would I forever be reminded of kneeling beside him sobbing words of love, comfort, and encouragement while we waited for the ambulance?

The walls of our home muffled the sound of a single gunshot. They absorbed our screams of horror, our sobs of anguish and cries of despair. But those walls also echoed years of giggles from five mischievous children, whoops of delight on Christmas mornings, shared confidences, fears, and dreams and, of course, disagreements, disciplines, tears of disappointment and frustration. A closet door frame recorded fourteen years of each child's growth. A fully grown but crownless fir tree in the front yard reminded us of the wish of a five year old to have his very own Christmas tree the year we moved in. The corner rock and flower garden, designed and planted by the son who ended his life, could be viewed from the kitchen window; the makeshift basement theater that entertained captive friends and family on winter Sunday afternoons; the orange cupboards in the garage that illustrated the risk of not being color-specific when asking two disgruntled teenage brothers to paint the cupboards with "whatever there is enough of"—all were part of our home, our lives, our family history.

Homes are memory generators. I am a symbolic memory collector and develop emotional attachment to places where meaningful, especially happy, life events take place. Our memories make up the tapestry of our lives, good memories or bad. When we move we take them with us, good memories and bad. But we don't take with us the places where memories were made. For some this is a blessing. Others will experience a move as another major loss.

My husband and I were fortunate to have been advised that intense grief impairs judgment and that making a major life-altering change within the first year could result in an irreversible mistake. We decided to stay in our home for at least a few months, not because it was prudent but because we did not have the energy to do otherwise. With the help of family and friends we installed carpet, rearranged the furniture, and replaced pictures in the room where our son had ended his life. It was still the same room but it had a different look and feel. At first it was barely tolerable. As we got used it, the room became acceptable and, eventually, a comfortable part of our home again.

As a forty-eight-year-old adult, Jim told of his mother's decision to move the family to another state a short time after his father's suicide when Jim was ten years old. They left behind all that was familiar and all the friends and neighbors who had known them as a family. Because the move was to be a fresh start, the children were instructed not to speak of the manner of their father's death to anyone in their new location. While the move insulated the family from being asked uncomfortable questions, it also isolated them from people who were part of their family history. They lost a point of reference that would have been comforting, grounding, even reassuring. They lost the community where they didn't have to explain their father's absence and where they might have, at some time, discussed their father's death as a family unit.

As you contemplate the need to move and deliberate the pros and cons with your family you may wish to consider some of the following questions.

Will making a move be even more disruptive and painful for the majority of family members? Your family has suffered a terrible loss. Will relocating create yet another loss that necessitates adjustment and requires forming new relationships during a time of emotional upheaval? If the family has a happy history in this home, a move will probably be an emotional hardship. If time spent in this house was full of conflict and unhappiness, the surviving family may benefit considerably from starting fresh in a new location.

Is the prospect of living in the present residence intolerable and out of the question? Or can you continue to live there for a few weeks, six months, a year? Selling one's house is a major, life-altering decision. Once property is sold it belongs to someone else. If you feel threatened and uncomfortable in the house but are unsure about letting it go, is it possible or practical to lease the house to a reliable party or even allow it to remain vacant for a few months? These options allow some healing space that may lend a different perspective and not require you to make a major decision when you are not at your decision-making best.

Will a move add to or relieve financial burdens? Household income may decide this issue for you. However, should you decide to sell your home, it is prudent to rely upon a reputable real estate agent who will protect your interests and relieve you of the emotional tedium of "just lookers" and can bargain with potential purchasers. An agent can arrange for repairs or redecorating that will help you get the best price for your home.

Will relocating mean a change of school for the children? A longer drive to work? Will a move isolate or distance you from your major support sources, separate the children from their caring friends? Or will it bring you nearer to extended family; to comfortable, familiar surroundings where you can share your loss and be reinforced in your grief, have help with the children, and be able to talk with someone who also shared a positive history with the person who died?

Is the decision to move a consensus among family members? The loss has been suffered by the entire household. If a move is made, the entire household moves. To minimize future conflict, strive for an amicable consensus. Share facts with children at their level of understanding, allow family members to express their feelings, to listen to explanations and participate in discussions of why the move is necessary. Too often, sometimes years later, surviving children and siblings, even spouses and parents, express resentment that their feelings or wishes were not considered in matters concerning themselves or the family. Their sense of helplessness, injustice, and loss was magnified by not having a voice in major family decisions.

Is this a practical move due to downsizing need? When children no longer live at home and there is no need for lots of space, downsizing may be in order. Many retired couples look forward to this time of less yard work, less housework and less expense. But for others, moving from a home that holds emotional attachment, even a house too big and too expensive, can be traumatic and frightening. This may be especially true if a life-shattering event, such as a family member's death, occurred in the house. How does one manage the conflict between being more practical and being reluctant to let go of a specific place? Many people find themselves in this kind of conflict between leaving the old and familiar behind and adapting to the new and unknown. To ease this transition you may wish to take lots and lots of pictures with notations on the album pages so you will remember happy, even sad, times in each room. You may choose to use a movie camera to make a virtual tour of the old home. Letting go has many facets, and moving is one of them.

In early acute grief we feel anxious and restless, desperate to find a more comfortable emotional place for ourselves. Usually we are surrounded by loving people who, just as desperately, want to help us find that more comfortable place by giving us advice. This pulls us one way and another at the worst possible time. If you have the luxury of time, with no great urgency about making a decision, discuss the To Move or Not to Move question with a trusted friend who has no emotional or financial investment in your decision, one who will help you weigh what is best for you, your family, and your individual circumstances. This may be your legal or financial advisor, your clergyman, a counselor, or a member of your extended family. Ultimately, the decision must be for the long-term benefit of the entire household.

Be gentle with yourself, dear survivor. After you have explored practical options and the decision to move has been made, don't belabor or second guess it. Be confident that you have made the best possible decision for yourself and those you love, then view the move as a positive step and look to the future with hope.

Life Insurance and Suicide

"Learn from yesterday. Live for today. Hope for tomorrow."

Albert Einstein

When our children were born, my husband purchased small life insurance policies for each of them. The premiums were low and the coverage was small but enough to cover burial expense should such an unthinkable tragedy occur. After our son's death, my husband filed a claim for our son's insurance benefits. I found the word *benefits* abhorrent. How insensitive and cruel to imply we, his parents, would profit from his death! The term *compensation* would have been more palatable. And what were we to do with any money remaining after our son's funeral expenses were paid? Since we were fortunate enough not to need the money for life's necessities, as can be the case when a breadwinner dies, we placed it in trust at our church with the intent of eventually funding suicide prevention education for youth.

The belief that suicide invalidates life insurance is widespread, and from interaction with suicide bereaved I learned that many who collect life insurance are deeply conflicted by the cause of death and payment. Be assured, dear survivor, that people rarely purchase life insurance with the intent of killing themselves wait the one or two years required for the policy to take effect, and then end their lives. Life insurance is purchased to provide for the loved ones left behind, regardless of the cause of death. Survivors often desperately need the insurance money to care for themselves, their children, or other family members yet may be very uncomfortable because, as one young widow stated, "insurance money, in exchange for my husband's death, seems tainted." The purchase of life insurance is a responsible, caring transaction that allows the policyholder peace of mind knowing his/her family will not be further deprived should he/she die prematurely. Although a life insurance payment may be difficult to receive, try to find comfort by viewing it as a loving gift from the person who has died.

The rather dry paragraphs that follow describe the history of life insurance and, specifically, how early life insurance companies protected policyholders against adverse selection in the event of death by suicide and at the same time made provisions for financial support to bereaved families following suicide. To ease the way for survivors-after-suicide beneficiaries, I have included explanations, definitions of various types of insurance coverage, directions for filing a claim, and encouragement to gratefully accept the support thoughtfully provided you.

In the United States, life insurance originated in eighteenth-century fraternal organizations. One benefit offered by many early brotherhoods was the option of contributing money to a mutual trust to be proportionately distributed to the contributing member's family after his death. To protect the trust from a contributor placing his family at unfair advantage by killing himself, suicide was discouraged by denying these families any disbursement from the trust.

In the founding years of the life insurance industry, suicide claims were almost totally excluded. A few policies did allow such claims when the suicide was the result of insanity, but establishing the dividing line between sane and insane suicides proved extremely difficult and controversial.

Around the turn of the twentieth century the industry began to recognize the injustice of excluding suicide completely, for this practice punished innocent families and went against the basic purpose of life insurance, which was to provide for dependents upon the death of the family wage earner. But making no mention of suicide admitted the possibility of "adverse selection against the company": an individual purchasing life insurance with the intent of killing himself, yet assuring the financial well-being of his family. The directors feared this possibility might even be viewed as an inducement to suicide. A compromise clause within the life insurance contract excluded payment to survivors of suicide for a specific period. After the specified term, the suicide's beneficiary, upon making claim, would be paid the policy's face value, the same as any other death. Should the policyholder end his life before the term was fulfilled, the beneficiary who made a claim would be returned all premiums paid, with or without interest, depending on the terms of the contract.

The term of exclusion is regulated by the laws of the state in which the policy is written. The term begins on the date of policy issue or the effective date (which, typically, are one and the same), unless adverse medical history or hazardous occupation or avocation prohibits immediate binding. A life insurance company has the option of specifying a lesser term than provided by the state. Most states require the term of exclusion be limited to two years. However, Colorado (Colorado Statute 10-7-109) and North Dakota (Section 26.1-33-05 "Provisions required in life insurance" subsection 12) limit the term of exclusion to one year. Missouri prohibits any specified term excluding an insurer from risk of suicide in policies written in that state (Missouri Revised Statutes, Chapter 376, section 376.620). To exclude payments in the event of suicide, a Missouri insurer must prove that life insurance was purchased in contemplation of suicide. As it is impossible in most cases to prove intent of this kind, the effect of the Missouri law is to nullify the suicide provision of life insurance policies issued in that state.

Upon applying for permanent life insurance (also known as whole life insurance) an individual may purchase a rider paying his beneficiary multiples of the policy's face value should the insured die accidentally. Accidental death is defined as resulting from unexpected and/or violent external means independent of any other cause, with both cause and result being unforeseeable. Since suicide is intentional, the cause is not from external means, nor is the resulting death unforeseen or unexpected; therefore, multiple indemnities are not payable.

In deaths whose cause is undetermined but could be either accident or suicide, there is always a strong presumption *against* suicide because of the inherent love of life and the instinct for self-preservation.

State laws regulate the insurance industry to safeguard the policyholder's investment. But some of the protective provisions also offer a remote possibility that death benefits will be unclaimed by beneficiaries unaware of a policy's extended value. Suicide beneficiaries, intimidated by myths of life insurance being invalidated by suicide, may fail to claim benefits. After five to seven years, the accumulated cash value of unclaimed benefits is placed in state custody and is usually retrievable.

Upon discovering insurance documents, regardless of dates and exclusions, the beneficiary or his/her representative should request a policy coverage review from the insurance company. Any beneficiary in doubt as to a policy's value, whether it is in force, or whether the term of exclusion has been met, should file a claim (with each claim accompanied by a death certificate). Since, as previously stated, an insurance company has the option of specifying a lesser term of exclusion, it is not inconceivable that an insurance company would waive the few days lacking to meet the exclusion term, especially a term of two years. Making a claim against a policy that is not in force *does not* constitute fraud. If the policy terms have not been met or it is not in force, the claimant will receive written notice from the insurance company simply stating the policy is not in force and no settlement will be forthcoming.

In contesting an insurance settlement, beneficiaries are well advised to protect their interest with legal counsel expert in the area of dispute. It is not necessary, however, to engage an attorney to file a claim for life insurance benefits. Upon notifying the company of a policyholder's death, the beneficiary may complete the "form of claimant" as received or ask assistance from the insurer's local representative. In disputes over insurance benefits, the coroner's opinion and death certificates are not necessarily decisive. Insurance policies are civil contracts and the final determination of payment is made by the court. Any grievance concerning claim settlement procedure should be filed with the state insurance commissioner's office.

The factor that defines death as suicide rather than accident is intention. Clarifying a victim's pre-death intent typically involves a psychological autopsy. This process is the effort to reconstruct the details of the victim's life situation, behavior, and the events preceding the death by interviews with persons close to the deceased. This circumstantial data, a psychological autopsy, combined with the facts of the anatomical autopsy and police reports of the death scene, are reviewed by the court in determining the mode of death.

Most disputes are settled out of court by negotiation. In the few that go to trial, after the adversaries present their respective versions of the facts and the court balances the credibility of the various witnesses' testimony, the judge directs the jury to arrive at a verdict regarding the decedent's intent.

Severe financial reverses may be viewed as a contributing factor in suicide, and they also make it likely that the insured has defaulted on life insurance premiums. An individual permanent life insurance contract typically protects the policyholder with a reinstatement privilege allowing a policy lapsed for non-payment to be reinstated within three to five years by paying back premiums and proving insurability. Once the insurer accepts the policy as reinstated, the conditions of the original contract are revived, and the term of exclusion specified in the suicide clause does not begin anew.

The individual permanent life insurance contract also includes a non-forfeiture provision for the policyholder's protection. After the grace period expires, the policyholder is advised that the policy is in lapse and is offered the option to:

1. Surrender the policy in exchange for the accumulated cash value or

2. Convert the accumulated cash value into a permanent paid-up policy of reduced value or

3. Convert the accumulated cash value into a face-value policy for an extended term.

When the policyholder does not select any of these options, the investment is automatically protected by conversion to either a permanent paid-up policy of reduced value or a face-value policy for an extended term.

Term insurance is quite another matter. Term insurance is purchased to meet contingencies of a definite and temporary period and is convertible or renewable only by contract provision. Term insurance offers no grace period, no non-forfeiture provision, and no cash value. The day the purchased term ends, the protection ends.

Nearly all group life insurance is renewable term insurance. Once the group life insurance becomes effective for a full-time employee, the protection continues as long as the employee remains in the service of the employer. When employment terminates, the group life coverage typically extends thirty-one days beyond the date of termination, and any death occurring within that time is payable. Most group insurance is convertible to a permanent form of life insurance during this extension period, but only about 3 percent is ever converted. In all convertible forms of insurance, the exclusion term in the suicide clause is effective from the date of the original policy.

Is workmen's compensation payable for the ultimate reaction to job-related stress, suicide?

Resolution of each situation is based upon the circumstances surrounding the individual case. Examples:

(a) In New York State a lawyer's who had overwhelming financial responsibilities was subjected to additional pressures by the death of his father. After making what he considered to be a serious error in the workplace, he killed himself. The court directed workmen's compensation be paid to his widow, citing job-related stress as a precipitating factor in his death.

(b) During a newspaper strike in another state a striking pressman, depressed by increasing indebtedness, ended his life. The court determined the precipitating stress was non-work-related because at the time of his death the man was not actively involved in promoting the interest of his employer. His widow was denied compensation. These cases indicate that court decisions are based on proof of causation: harassment, intimidation, undue pressure of unrealistic deadlines imposed by superiors or management, or other stress-provoking work conditions beyond normal wear and tear.

Lost policy search

The beneficiary of a missing policy may still collect. The beneficiary must contact various companies in search of the carrier. After obvious insurers have been contacted and no policy has been found, the search may be continued through the American Council of Life Insurance.

Does suicide in the family jeopardize the insurability of other family members?

A life insurance policy is a unique contract between insurer and insured, tailored to meet the needs of the purchaser and the eventual needs of his/her beneficiary. An insurer's willing-ness to contract with a client cannot legally be affected by a previous suicide in the family.

Does mental illness affect insurability?

Typically, a life insurance application does not ask if the proposed insured has ever been treated for mental illness, ner-vous breakdown, depression or other disorder of the brain or nervous system. It is advisable for anyone who has received psychiatric treatment, i.e. following bereavement or other emotional trauma, to protect their insurability with a written statement from the physician citing the reason for treatment and its successful conclusion or prognosis.

A policyholder's suicide will be a horrifying, traumatic expe-rience for the surviving family, but a claim for a suicidal death is neither unique nor a matter of curiosity to the claim proces-sor. The recipient of life insurance payment, when the cause of death is suicide, can expect the same courteous, expedient claim settlement as the beneficiary of any other cause of death.

Many recipients of life insurance settlements have an aver-sion, as I did, to the terms *benefit and beneficiary.* To some family survivors, wording implying they have benefited from the death of a loved one is so repugnant as to cause delays in filing claims or spending the settlement, especially when the cause of death is suicide. Recipients of policy settlements fol-lowing suicide may find some peace of mind knowing their deceased loved one purchased the policy out of concern for the financial well-being of beloved family members long before making the decision to end his/her life . . . at least one or two years before.

A small lump-sum is paid by the Social Security Administration upon the death of a person who has worked long enough to be insured under the Social Security program. The lump-sum death benefit can be paid upon the death of the insured person even if they were not receiving retirement or disability benefits at the time of death.

The one-time payment goes to the surviving spouse if he or she was living with the beneficiary at the time of death, or, if living apart, was eligible for Social Security benefits on the beneficiary's earnings record for the month of death. If there is no surviving spouse, the payment is made to a child who was eligible for benefits on the beneficiary's earnings record in the month of death. If no spouse or child meeting these requirements exists, then the lump sum will not be paid. The lump sum death payment cannot be paid directly to funeral homes for funeral expenses.

Social Security should be notified as soon as possible after a person has died. To learn more about Social Security benefits, who is eligible, and how to apply for them visit the website: www.ssa.gov or call 1-800-772-1213.

Disclaimer: Information regarding life insurance and suicide, researched through Shepard's Citations (LexisNexis) various life insurance companies, and other Internet sources, is not to be construed or accepted as legal advice or determination, but should be verified by your insurance company representative, the Insurance Commissioner in your state, and/or by your legal advisor.

Marital Intimacy Following a Child's Suicide

"Grief knits two hearts in closer bond than happiness ever can; and common sufferings are far stronger links than common joy."

Alphonse de Lamartine

The death of a child wreaks havoc in the lives of the surviving parents. It may wreak havoc in the intimacy of the marriage as well. Sexual intimacy and performance after a couple's child ends his/her life may be greatly affected, sometimes because of assumptions about responsibility. Intimacy will be even more affected if the child died in the family home, in the parent's bedroom, or following parental disagreement regarding issues perceived as a contributing factor to the death.

Resuming marital intimacy depends to some extent upon the couple's sexual activity and habits prior to the child's death and even more so upon the importance of physical lovemaking to their marriage. Some of the questions asked by surviving parents: How soon does intimacy resume after one's child dies? Is having sexual intercourse soon after the death of one's child disrespectful, disgusting, and abominable? Does resuming sexual activity depend upon the age of the child at the time of his/her death? Does the cause of the child's death impact sexual intimacy? Will we ever be sexually compatible again?

Very little has been written about sexual intimacy following the death of someone close, and some readers may wonder if, in fact, there is reason to address the issue at all. I am persuaded to do so because several surviving parents have inquired, and some have shared experiences regarding their intimate lives that caused them concern and conflict after their child's suicide.

Judith told of being appalled when her husband made sexual overtures a couple weeks following the suicide of their thirty-year-old son. "Fortunately, I didn't show my shock and revulsion," she said. "I sensed his need was for comfort and closeness and an outlet for his tremendous emotional pain. Our coupling was by no means joyous, gratifying, or on any previous level of satisfaction and was over very quickly. I knew I had been right in not showing distaste when, immediately afterward, he tearfully apologized for being so insistent and insensitive. It may have been one of a few times when our desire for closeness was not mutual and perhaps the only time in our many years of marriage when he was not considerate of my wishes and feelings. I understood and accepted his need to join with me as yet another means of expressing his feelings, his despair and pain."

Judith continued, "While it was many, many months before our lovemaking regained any semblance of normalcy or pleasure, I recognized that sexual intimacy could be an expression of grief as well as an opportunity to give and receive comfort and reassurance. Perhaps, in this situation, it is the deepest and most fundamental expression of grief and love."

A bereaved father shared his deep hurt at his wife's continued withdrawal many months after their son's suicide. She wanted no touching, no tenderness, no physical exchange of any kind. She was repulsed by any advances from him, declaring his wish for intimacy to be disrespectful to their son's memory. He was desolate, feeling as if he had lost her as well as losing his son.

Marital intimacy is very private communication between partners who have learned mutually satisfying ways of expressing love, passion, tenderness, and even hurt. The ultimate expression of being married is intimacy—physical, intellectual, and emotional. I once read that stress sex following a child's death is not unusual and may well be the surviving parent's unspoken effort to recapture the safety of the pre-death marriage, albeit briefly.

Cuddling, stroking, tenderness, and, yes, coitus, can provide great solace. The catharsis of openly communicating with one's spouse through touch, look, action, or word regarding feelings surrounding the death is healing, especially when communication is by mutual consent and the suicide is not the sole topic.

Open communication between parents after their child's death is important. Sharing feelings with the one person who understands the magnitude of this loss is a powerful catharsis and a means of renewed emotional bonding. Both parents may need to speak again and again of what has happened and repeatedly recount all the circumstances surrounding the death. They will need reassurance as to one another's well-being, and both will need to speak of their own pain and fears.

It is likely that there will come a time when one parent will not wish or need to verbally reprocess the death situation with the intensity or frequency that characterized the early days of their mourning. But the other partner may still need the more intense degree of exchange. At a time when emotions are very fragile this discrepancy can be devastating to the one who still needs to process the death and frustrating to the partner who feels the need to move on. This is especially true when one partner is a recent stepparent who has not formed a deep bond with the deceased child. He or she will be empathetic but likely will not experience as acute a sense of loss as the birth parent. A solution must be found that fits the needs of both parents. One couple's solution was an agreement to set aside an hour every day to discuss their child's death and their grief; both would participate in the conversation. When the hour had passed, they would turn their conversation to events of the day, their mutual love of the outdoors and sports, watch a television show, take a walk, read, or focus on various hobbies.

It was difficult in the beginning. The mother had so much she wanted to speak of again and again. The father felt nothing was being gained by rehashing the events surrounding the death. But they held fast to their agreement. The mother continued to attend a support group alone where she could further meet her need to speak of her child's death. Within a few weeks the daily hour began to include other topics of mutual interest and then became an hour three or four times a week. The mother continued to need to speak more and oftener of her child's death than the father but she found other avenues of expression, comfort, and understanding. The father's willingness to actively participate in an hour of discussion validated the mother's needs even though they were not his own. The compromise of these parents seems very wise. It provided a healthy outlet for their pain as well as a foundation for building additional common interests. Acquiring shared knowledge about the death, the dynamics of suicide, and the peculiarities of suicide bereavement can lend a level of integrity to the grief and acceptance of the loss that more closely binds the relationship.

On all levels, intimacy reassures the bereaved partners that their love is strong and their marriage enduring. The parents' world has been shattered by the suicide death of their child, their lives are filled with the desperate craziness of grief, and any happiness in the future is unimaginable. Tender lovemaking offers grieving parents the comfort of closeness, safety, trust, hope, and gentle healing. Maintaining marital intimacy is an invaluable component in the emotional and physical well-being of both partners and in the future solidarity of the marriage.

About Divorce

*"What else is love but understanding and rejoicing
in the fact that another person lives, acts and experiences
otherwise than we do."*

Friedrich Nietzsche, *Human, All Too Human*

It is commonly believed that a great number of marriages collapse following the death of a child. This is not true. The death of a child is considered one of the deepest psychic wounds a parent can suffer, which may be the basis for the misconception that a huge proportion of marriages end after a child dies.

According to Cis Dickson, one of the co-founders of the Grief Center of Texas, fifty-four parents whose children had died nearly all told interviewers that their marriage was more secure, that their relationship with their mate became closer and stronger as they grieved the death of their child together.

A support organization for bereaved parents, the Compassionate Friends, surveyed parents through questionnaires regarding the impact of their child's death upon their marriage. The results, available on the Compassionate Friends web site do not show a high rate of divorce among parents who have had a child die: 72 percent of parents who were married at the time of their child's death were still married at the time of the survey. Only 12 percent of the marriages ended in divorce. (In the other marriages, one spouse had died.) Of the 12 percent that divorced, only one out of four, or 3 percent of the respondents to the survey, felt that the impact of their child's death contributed to the marriage's breakup.

These are relatively small samples, and I have found no broad statistics correlating a child's suicide with the parents' marriage or divorce. However, in my interactions with hundreds of surviving parents, I have seen few instances of divorce as a direct result of a child's suicide, perhaps even fewer than the 3 percent cited in the Compassionate Friends study. Interviews with numerous parents bereaved by suicide reveal great determination and effort to keep the surviving family unit intact. The benefit of therapy after a child's suicide cannot be ignored.

One parent who did divorce after her son ended his life answered the question whether the suicide death played a part in her divorce from her son's father. "Absolutely not! Our divorce was something that should have occurred years before he died but because of our religion and fear of family disapproval we continued a marriage that was very flawed and unhappy."

A factor in the rate of divorce among the parents of children who died by suicide may be the age of the child when he/she died. Suicide among children under age twelve is rare, and it is not unlikely that parents bereaved by a young child's suicide seek counseling immediately. Parents bereaved by the suicide of an adolescent and particularly an adult child may recognize that there were many factors at work in their child's life that had little or nothing to do with the environment in which their son or daughter was reared, somewhat lessening the chance of blaming one another or suffering blame from others.

Too frequently the surviving parents of an adult child fix the blame for the suicide upon their child's spouse, compounding the grief of the surviving husband or wife. Blaming the spouse deprives both the parents and the surviving spouse of uniting in their bereavement. The conflict and anger complicate the grieving process and are very destructive to surviving children of the deceased. Irreversible damage can be done to surviving relationships before the parent survivor accepts the fact that no marriage partner has the power to cause the other to deliberately end his/her life. Even though the marriage may have been unhappy, even toxic and abusive, there are many ways of dissolving a relationship other than ending one's own life.

Surrogate Parenting

"It takes a village to raise a child."

African Proverb

When a youth's suicide leaves behind grieving parents and young siblings, or a parent's suicide leaves young children, a temporary interruption in parenting can occur. The bereaved parent/s may be so overwhelmed by the death, the cause of death and the resulting grief that they are emotionally, physically, and mentally unable to meet the needs of their surviving grief-stricken children. It is not that the parents deliberately abdicate their parental responsibilities, but they are so consumed by the pain of their loss they cannot provide the parenting their young surviving children need at a time when they need it most. This parenting void may go on for months. Bereaved parents tell of being on automatic pilot for at least a year and of having little memory of involvement with their surviving children during that time.

On the other hand, the surviving children, believing that they should not impose their own grief, loss, and reaction to their sibling or parent's suicide upon their anguished parent/s, may stifle expression of their grief and their concerns about their future and the future of the family. Repressing these feelings may lead to long-range effects of unresolved grief; the children may seek unhealthy and inappropriate ways of coping or belonging; they may misinterpret the parents' apathy and grief as lack of caring. A surviving sibling told of wanting to shout to her parents, "Hey! What about me. I hurt too. And I'm still here. I didn't kill myself."

Andrea was sixteen when her brother ended his life. She felt that she not only had lost her brother, her only sibling, but had lost her parents as well. "Oh, they were there. They hugged me and asked if I was doing OK and if I wanted to talk, but they seemed off in their own world, absent and disconnected from me and my feelings. Sometimes I felt as if I didn't matter anymore, that they had lost the child they loved the most. Other times they wouldn't let me out of their sight. I guess they were afraid something would happen to me, or that I would kill myself. My dad and mom were really heartbroken for a long time. They cried when we talked about J. D. I didn't want to make them cry so I didn't tell them how much I missed him and I didn't want to make them feel worse by having them see me cry or by dumping my problems on them. So I pretty much kept my feelings to myself."

Andrea continued, "It was like my world came to an end when my brother died. I was really alone. There was nowhere safe anymore. Nothing was the same. Nobody understood. There was stuff going on for me, things I was struggling with before J. D. died that were still there after he died, only I wasn't able to deal with them as well and he wasn't there to talk to. There was no one I could talk to except my girlfriend Janie and her mother. Her mother was really great. Janie's baby sister had been almost a year old when she died of SIDS. Janie's mom helped me understand that having a child die leaves such a big hole in a parent's heart that, for a long time afterward, their energy and interest in other facets of their life sort of leaks out that hole. They just go through the motions of living because their grieving leaves them exhausted and empty and unable to see anything but what they have lost. That doesn't mean they don't care about the children they have left because those children are now even more precious. Janie's mom didn't know my mom very well but she called mom now and then and always reminded me to call my parents when I was at Janie's house.

"The spring prom was only eight weeks after my brother's suicide. A really cool guy asked me to go. It gave me something to be happy about but when I told my mom she kind of looked through me and said, 'Oh, that's nice, dear.' Janie's mom called my mom and asked if she could take me to shop for a dress and didn't my mom want to go too. The four of us went prom dress shopping. Mom told me how grown-up and pretty I looked. We had lunch. It was a good time. It made me feel like part of a family again. It reminded me that mom really did care. I think it helped mom a little too."

When family dynamics like these are present, it may be prudent to seek support from a trusted friend or member of the extended family to serve as a surrogate parent to the surviving children. The role of the surrogate is to help meet the needs of the grieving children by allowing them to talk of their brother, sister or parent's death, their feelings about it, and to be alert to destructive social or academic behaviors. The surrogate reassures the children, guards their well-being, suggests counseling to the parents if alarming indicators warrant it, attends school activities if the parent is unable, or reminds the parents of events important to the child, even assuming some of the parenting responsibility until the parents adjust their emotional equilibrium and can resume their parenting roles.

Surrogates do for a grieving family what friends, neighbors and extended family provide during other kinds of crises—illness, incapacitation, military deployment, and the like. Surrogates need not be just one person, and a surrogate is not exactly a substitute parent; he or she is a stand-in or standby. Surrogates are caring people who perform parenting duties until the parent is strong enough to again resume and fulfill parenting obligations and responsibilities.

MISSING PIECES

Bits and Pieces

"Knowledge is power."

Sir Francis Bacon, *Sacred Meditations*

Is suicide a crime?

Suicide is not a crime. Because suicide is an unnatural death, there is an investigation to determine whether or not the death was self-inflicted. Law enforcement often temporarily confiscates computers, weapons, diaries, writing, and anything relevant to determining the cause of death. The investigation and confiscation of items may cause the bereaved to believe it is because suicide is a criminal act. There is no statute in any state in the United States under which suicide is a crime. Nor is there a state in which attempting suicide is a crime. In most states, however, assisting suicide is a crime. If someone assists in a suicide by providing a weapon or administering a fatal dose of drugs, the appropriate charge is murder. Suicide was a crime in England and Wales until 1961.

Completed suicide versus committed suicide

Many suicide bereaved find the term *completed suicide* less harsh and threatening, more tolerable than the common term *committed suicide*, which implies a crime. Other survivors find the word completed abrasive and choose to say *died by suicide, died by her own hand*, or *intentionally ended his life.*

Suicide notes

It is estimated that no more than 20 percent of suicides leave notes. Suicide bereaved who have not been left a note may lament that fact, believing that suicide notes tell why the death occurred. Because suicide notes are most often written when the victim is not in a rational state of mind, the contents of the note usually reveal little, certainly nothing that satisfactorily explains the reason behind the act. 'Take care of my dog," "Sorry about the mess," "Forgive me. I love you all" are actual suicide notes. Occasionally a note blaming a family member adds to the chaos and anguish. In such an instance, the family must consider that nearly all suicide notes are written in an irrational state of mind and should be viewed as the distorted perception of the deceased at that time.

Sometimes there are successive suicides within a family. Does this mean suicide is inherited?

Suicide is not inherited. The tendency toward mental disorders does run in families just as the tendency toward physical illnesses such as cancer and heart disease runs in families. Suicide can also be a learned behavior, a means of coping with pain and/or solving problems, exemplified by family members who have ended their life.

How should suicide bereaved answer insensitive questions?

Suicide bereaved are never obliged to relieve anyone's curiosity, but well-meaning people will ask questions. Decide upon what you want to give as a direct answer rather than fumbling between the truth and "it isn't any of your business." If a new acquaintance learns of my son's death and asks the cause I may tell them, "He died of an injury." The fact that it was a deliberately self-inflicted gunshot injury is personal and I treat it as such. If I choose to share this with others, I do. If I choose not to, I don't. It has nothing to do with secrecy and everything to do with privacy. The attitude of the inquirer usually depends upon how I answer their question. If the individual asking questions seems morbidly curious I may end the conversation by saying, "This is too painful for me to discuss." As the years pass and my knowledge of grief and suicide broadens, I usually simply state, "My son took his own life." This can result in a teachable moment; it might encourage the inquirer to express concern for a friend or family member, which can provide me an opportunity to inform or refer.

What do I do when people makes jokes about suicide?

There will always be people who express the intensity of their feelings by exclaiming, "Oh, I could just shoot myself!" These people are not at risk of ending their lives and probably have no inkling of the impact of such a statement upon a person bereaved by suicide. When this kind of statement is made in my presence I may ignore it. Often I exercise the option of replying, "Suicide is never a laughing matter" or "There is nothing funny about suicide."

How does one confront suicide-related advertisements, television sitcom jokes, or suicide-promoting music and videos?

I am deeply offended by efforts to sell products or raise program ratings by using suicide as a theme or laugh line. As a survivor of a loved one's suicide, I believe it is my responsibility to confront efforts to commercialize or profit from using suicide as a topic. To do nothing lends acceptance to jesting about a very serious health problem. When I see suicide used in such a manner I write to the sponsor, advise them that their show or commercial is offensive because of the use of suicide as a joke or theme, tell them why I feel that way, and emphatically advise them that because of their tasteless selection of material I will no longer watch their show or purchase their product. With the Internet providing easy access to support groups and suicide prevention centers all over the country, an offensive theme or phrase seldom escapes notices and often creates an outpouring of protest to producers and sponsors. Any survivor can and should voice such objections.

What is a psychological autopsy?

Some deaths require a psychological autopsy to determine the exact mode of death. A psychological autopsy is a retrospective reconstruction of the life history of the decedent, examining physical, psychological, and environmental details of the decedent's life in order to gain better knowledge of the death process and the victim's role in his own death. This analysis focuses upon the decedent's intention relating to his/her own death and is undertaken by mental health professionals, usually at the request of an authority agency. The obsessive review of suicide by the bereaved can share many of the investigative elements of a professional psychological autopsy.

How are suicide statistics compiled?

Vital statistics are calculated per 100,000 persons. At the end of each year, the county coroner's office sends death statistics to the state bureau of vital statistics. Death statistics are separated by cause of death. The bureau in each state determines whether the person who died by suicide was a resident of that state. A resident of a state (i.e. Iowa) who ended his/her life in another state (i.e. Colorado) is counted by the state of residency (Iowa), not the state in which the death occurred (Colorado), which would count it only as rate of incident. The final statistical determination takes about eighteen months. It has been estimated that each suicide intimately affects at least six other people.

For suicide statistics in the United States visit www.suicidology.org and click on statistics.

Searching For Answers

"I don't know why. I'll never know why. I don't like it. I don't have to like it. What I do have to do is make a choice about my living. What I want to do is accept it and go on living. The choice is mine."

Iris Bolton, *My Son, My Son*

When someone we love dies, we look to a physician, to law enforcement, or to some other authority for an explanation. We hope for a justifiable reason, a definable cause because we want to understand why the death occurred and to accept the permanent absence of this beloved person.

When someone we love has deliberately ended his/her life there is no physician to explain the progress of a life-terminating illness. There is no patrolman to trace the path of a head-on collision. There is no assailant upon which to heap the blame and vent our rage. But there has to be a reason! A cause! Some justification or explanation for this death and our loss! We are convinced if we only knew why this unfathomable decision was reached, we would have an easier acceptance of the death and our loss. And so begins our search for answers.

We physically search through every particle of their personal belongings, every scrap of their writing, every communication they received, hoping to find an explanation. We search verbally by talking with their close friends, peers, co-workers, with everyone who was in contact with them those last few days, hoping to piece together the puzzle of *why* such depth of despair could be reached unrecognized. We talk of our last time with them over and over, seeking revelation. We search through books and articles about suicide, sometimes seeing, in retrospect, what we had no awareness of before. We look back on the past, often bypassing the loving, reinforcing times to focus on neglects or hurts, blaming ourselves, seeing only our sins of omission or commission. Sometimes we seek spiritual answers, searching for how God views this death, our loved one, and ourselves.

Well-meaning friends may try to discourage our searching by telling us we are as close to the answer to *why* at the time of the death as we will ever be. This may be true, but the search for answers is a normal and necessary component to our healing. We need to know and to search for why this death occurred. We need to try to make sense of an act, a death, a loss that makes no sense to us and never will.

We search. The energy of the search and the lack of productivity exhaust us. We renew our efforts. We search and research. After this process is repeated many times, we resign ourselves to never finding anything that justifies the act of suicide. Finally, reluctantly, we accept that this death cannot be explained, defined, or justified. It will never make sense. We begin to realize that we are searching rationally for the cause of an irrational act. Reluctantly we accept the fact that this death is, and forever will be, inexplicable. The death **is**.

What benefit does the searching have, and how long does it take? It is through searching that we are reconciled to the fact of our loved one's death. It is through searching that we accept suicide as the cause. We hate it, but it's a fact that we must acknowledge and live with. And it is through searching that we eventually attain the understanding that why they died or how they died is not of primary importance. What will always be important is that their physical presence is forever gone from us. What we must do is resolve the indescribable pain of that separation. We must adapt our lives to the void created by their death.

The searching takes until we are no longer compelled by the need to search. It takes until we are ready and willing to invest the energy of the search into positive, productive action that helps us to heal and flourish. For each of us, my wounded friends, the search for answers takes as long as it takes.

The Obsessive Review

"God, grant me the serenity to accept
the things I cannot change,
The courage to change the things I can
and the wisdom to know the difference."

Reinhold Niebuhr, *The Serenity Prayer*

After the death of a loved one it is not unusual for the intimate mourners to find themselves mentally going over the last actions, the last words, the last contact with the person who has died. Especially when the death is violent or unexpected, those left behind search for what happened and why. This mental (cognitive) search is called the obsessive review. In the immediate aftermath of a death the obsessive review may occur unconsciously, robbing the bereaved of sleep and rest, often interrupting daytime concentration and conversation. The obsessive review differs from searching for answers. Searching for answers is an effort to learn *why it happened*. The obsessive review is striving to understand the events involving the deceased as they prepared for their death or *how it happened*.

Following the suicide of my son Kent, I repeatedly reviewed my failure to recognize and respond to his despair but I did not become deeply mentally involved in the steps he took to end his life. My review traveled far from his immediate past to his younger years, when he suffered the childhood hurts of being left out of schoolyard games. I recalled how inept he had been at sports and how he had longed for friends and acceptance. I looked back to his grade-school days when he was given an IQ test at my insistence after a teacher told me that I must accept that he was "slow." The test showed he had a genius level Intelligence Quotient. I remembered his reluctance to attend his first church camp and what fun he had there. I remembered him in *Sing Out America* and how proud he was of the demand for their performances; how thrilled we were by the beautiful music the choir made, their dancing and drills, and the pleasure it gave the audience. I recalled the day he told us he didn't have enough credits to graduate from high school, and his father and I meeting with his very indifferent counselor who admitted, with considerable surprise, that Kent was right, he did not have enough credits to graduate with his class. I recall the respect and pride I felt when, rather than give up, Kent returned to school to earn his diploma a year after his former classmates had graduated. I recalled his deteriorating confidence when he couldn't find work in a poor economy, of his disappointment at becoming ill with A/Victoria flu, missing so many classes he was unable to complete college semester courses, and his restored pride when he finally found a promising job.

The review of Kent's father was different, more immediate and more definitive of the term *obsessive review*. He suffered deeply as he focused on the steps Kent had taken, emotionally and physically, as he made his way toward the ending of his life. He mentally followed Kent as he took the shotgun from its case in the furnace room and, at some point, climbed a ladder to reach into the attic to find the shells. He felt Kent's pain and anxiety by mentally and emotionally visiting the time Kent's tears marked the paper as he wrote his final note telling us what great parents we were, how much he loved us all, how hard he had tried but how he believed his life wasn't worth the effort and pain it took to live. My husband mentally visualized and emotionally suffered every step Kent would have taken until he pulled the trigger.

Caring friends and extended family often discourage the effort of suicide bereaved to search, examine, or discover events preceding the death, engaging in the obsessive review. Those who offer this discouragement are well-meaning people who have no understanding of the need suicide bereaved have to understand how the death of a beloved person occurred. They wish to hurry us toward a more comfortable, perhaps safer, place. There are tears and trauma in reviewing events that led up to the death, but there can be healing.*

The obsessive review is a uniquely personal journey. What I can review and discard as being irrelevant may be of great relevance to another family member. For each of us, it is this personal, painful journey that allows us to accept and reconcile to what cannot be changed.

CAUTION: Any survivor who is or has been suicidal, who relates too closely to the steps toward death taken by the deceased or who continuously engages in the obsessive review may be in harm's way and should see a mental health professional.

PEACE

Self-Care

"Self-love, my liege, is not so vile a sin as self neglecting."

William Shakespeare, *Henry V,* Act II, Scene 4

Grieving is very hard work. It depletes energy and robs one of rest, of joy, and of the wish to care properly for oneself. For a time, most bereaved don't care whether they reestablish routine or restore structure in their lives. Some may not care about maintaining their health. Each is obsessed with the death and the loss that has occurred. Nothing seems more important than what has happened. Yet maintaining good health is critical to healthy grieving; to progressing on our grief journey; to establishing the necessary "new normal" that eventually allows us to love life again. As a self-care reminder, I include an acronym shared with me by a friend shortly after my son's death. My friend, a recovering alcoholic, told me this tool is used by persons with addictive disorders to help them maintain sobriety from day to day, hour to hour. With adaptation it contains some good advice for nurturing ourselves as we mourn our loss.

H.A.L.T!!
DON'T ALLOW YOURSELF TO BECOME TOO....

Hungry. During acute grief we may not feel like eating, but it is a time our bodies most need good nutrition to function well, to endure the stress of grief, and to sustain us without the betrayal of a health breakdown when we are least able to cope with health problems. Some bereaved will experience the opposite feeling of being deprived and empty, a gnawing in the stomach that seems to signal hunger. This false appetite encourages eating too much, too "junky," too often. The long-term risk is weight gain without benefit of good nutrition.

Eat wisely. It may help to eat several smaller meals a day of an easily digestible balance of food that will fuel your body, satisfy hunger, and keep you from feeling bloated or lethargic. Avoid heavy, spicy food that can cause indigestion, heartburn, or gas. You have no time or energy to waste on an upset digestive system. If you feel the need for a snack, nibble on fruit rather than brownies, ice cream, or chips.

Keep hydrated. Water is the best hydrant. Sodas, artificially sweetened or caffeinated drinks, coffee, or tea may not be as effective. Alcoholic drinks are depressants and should be ingested very sparingly or avoided altogether during acute grief. Excessive stimulants such as chocolate and caffeinated drinks late in the day may disrupt sleep or contribute to restlessness.

See your physician for a complete physical in the early weeks of your mourning. Review with your doctor dosages of medication you are presently taking and discuss unusual or lingering physical distress you have noticed since your loss. During acute grief, when our minds are on overload, we can become confused or negligent about medication necessary to sustaining good health. You may wish to ask the physician to recommend a well-balanced diet and supplementary multivitamins. Discuss with your physician any stress-related illnesses or condition you have that could worsen during acute grief, such as asthma, ulcers, cancer, hypertension, heart disease, colitis, or a history of stroke.

Feed your spiritual self. Our wound reaches to the depth of our soul. The tragedy of suicide often causes feelings of betrayal, rejection, fear, and distrust. These feelings can distance us from our source of spiritual comfort and replenishment. Talk with your Divine Source about your loss, your fears for the future, your anger, or whatever weighs heaviest on your heart at that moment. It is not unusual for suicide survivors to question their faith, declare they no longer believe in God, or express their anger at God for allowing the death to occur. It's OK to scream and rage at God. He understands our pain. God makes this journey with us; comforting us, loving us, healing us.

Angry. Not every bereaved person feels anger when a loved one dies, and that's normal. But to be angry after the death of someone we love is also normal. Anger is our protest against being deprived of the presence of our beloved. It may be directed toward ourselves for not having foreseen and prevented the death. It may be directed toward God for allowing the death to occur. There may be times that anger is displaced upon another family member. It is not uncommon for anger to be directed toward the person who ended their life. While anger is a normal emotion following a loved one's death, it is not normal or healthy to harbor it, to use it as a shield, to cling to it or fuel it until it grows into bitterness. Anger becomes unhealthy when the bereaved's thoughts are consumed by it and the words and actions of the bereaved reflect rage or thoughts of retribution.

Anger is energy. Channeled inward, anger can cause sleeplessness, irritability, depression, and irrational thoughts that have negative effects upon our physical and emotional well-being as well as upon those close to us. Our challenge is to transform anger into reconciliation to the cause the death and reshape our life around the void left by the death. We can transform anger by becoming informed about depression, suicide, and what the deceased was struggling with. We can manage anger by talking with clergy, therapists, or by taking anger management classes. We can exorcise anger through exercise: walking, running, hiking, biking, aerobics, tennis, racquetball, swimming, golf, or boxing. Exercise releases endorphins that enhance one's sense of well-being.

Lonely. A loved one has died. What was once part of our own life is now part of our past, our life in memory. The tremendous void can be overwhelming, causing us to feel isolated, to believe that no one could possibly understand our loss. There are times of deep despair and hopelessness. Learning that everyone who has grieved the death of a loved one has felt desperate, hopeless, and alone means little.

During times of acute loneliness, call a friend, talk with your clergy, ask someone to be with you for awhile, visit a neighbor, or write a letter to the one who has died. In your message tell them the things you would say if you could speak to them face to face—your hurt, your loneliness, of your fears, and your love. Many bereaved find great solace in journaling. Journaling provides sort of a mourning calendar. In months ahead, when you feel you have made little progress, you can review the journal to recognize and appreciate the growth and healing that has taken place.

We cannot change what has happened, but we can make choices that will help us reconcile to the loss and prepare us to live without the one who died. We can accept the offer of friends and family to visit, take us for a drive, or invite us for a meal. We can attend grief classes or support groups. We can read to gain some understanding of the grief process and how others coped. We can reach out to others who have experienced a deep grief and use our experience, growth, and understanding to help them and, thus, help ourselves.

Tired. Mourning is the hardest work we are ever called upon to do. We didn't seek it. We don't want it. We rebel against it. But the death of our loved one makes it ours. Mourning is exhausting, depleting our energy. During acute mourning we focus on our pain, our loss, and the past, often oblivious to what is taking place around us in the present and distorting our vision of the future. We must learn to pace ourselves in our grief work by becoming tired enough to rest well but without becoming overly tired and unable to gain restorative rest. It is prudent to postpone major decision-making when we are tired. We may need to take short naps. Good sleep revitalizes us and is imperative to our emotional and physical well-being.

Forgiveness

*"Without forgiveness life is governed by
an endless cycle of resentment and retaliation."*

Robert Assagioli, *Psychosynthesis*

Forgiveness may seem simple until we need to forgive following the death of someone dearly loved. A sea of unfamiliar emotions can make forgiveness impossible for a very long time. Until we forgive, as long as we harbor anger and resentment toward another, that person has power over us, preventing us from moving forward. Anger, until it is transformed into forgiveness, can fester into bitterness that corrodes the vessel that contains it and disfigures all that it touches.

If we are to achieve healthy measures of healing, we must eventually deal with forgiveness.

We may need to forgive ourselves for not being able to protect the beloved person or prevent their death.

We may need to forgive our loved one because of the way he or she died.

We may need to forgive doctors or counselors for failing to properly diagnose, cure, or save our loved one.

We need to forgive anyone— ourselves, our child, husband, wife, parent, sibling or any other person—who intentionally or unintentionally contributed to events that led to the death of our loved one.

We need to forgive those who fail to support us in our grief, those who make clueless or insensitive remarks, avoid mentioning our beloved's name or their death, or just stay away.

Forgiveness does not come easily or quickly but there is no time frame for forgiving.

Forgiveness does not change what has happened but it lifts a burden from our heart. It has been said that forgiveness is a gift we give ourselves. Forgiving frees us to heal, to love without fear, to live without bitterness, to be open to God's Grace and to know true peace in the future.

Mourning Tasks

"Mourning is not forgetting...It is an undoing. Every minute tie has to be untied and something permanent and valuable recovered and assimilated from the dust."

Margery Allingham

We have been sent on an unplanned journey. We didn't want or seek it but the suicide of someone dearly loved has made it ours. While our loss and grief are distinctly our own, there are tasks in common that suicide bereaved can perform in order to reach a peaceful plateau.

We must tell our story...again and again until we wear it out; until we don't need to tell it any more. It is in the telling that we grow slowly, reluctantly, toward the acknowledgment that the death and its cause are reality. It is in telling our story that we accustom ourselves to the word *suicide*, causing it to lose some of its power over us. It is in telling our story that this tragedy is woven into the fabric of our lives and becomes a part of who we are and will become—not uncommonly, a wiser, gentler, more compassionate person.

We must express our feelings...our anger, our fear, our sense of helplessness, our perceived responsibility or guilt, our longing and anguish and perhaps, for some bereaved, a sense of relief. All the emotions that build within must be expelled from our body. It is by expressing our emotions that we are relieved of some, that we cope with and resolve others. Our body and mind are not intended to retain the magnitude of tumultuous emotions we experience after the death of a beloved person. Trying to hold those feelings in can cause serious harm in the form of physical or emotional illness. Grief will have its way. The natural way is through expression—weeping, talking, reminiscing, exercising, therapy, whatever means works for us as long as it is not illegal and does not impose upon the grief or rights of others.

We must seek the truth. The chapter Search for Answers discusses our need to know why the death occurred and to search for any part we may have played in it. Suicide bereaved search for reasons, causes, justification for the death and their loss. They try to make sense of an act and resulting death that will never make sense. Seeking the truth is necessary, for it is in the seeking that we are finally reconciled to never having an answer, to never knowing why. It is by reconciling to never knowing why that we recognize we have to live without ever knowing why. And because we have to, we can and we do.

We must make meaning of the loss and give purpose to our grief. A part of our life and our future has been taken from us. The grief we experience from our loss has tremendous energy. There is great comfort and relief from investing grief energy into positive action. We do that by finding an energy receptacle or focus. Some of the most productive and successful safety campaigns were started by bereaved persons as memorials to their loved one and from determination that their loss be beneficial to others. Candice Lightner started Mothers Against Drunk Driving (MADD) after her thirteen-year-old daughter was killed by a car driven by a drunken driver. Nancy Brinker started Susan G. Komen for the Cure after making a vow to her sister dying of breast cancer. U.S. Senator Gordon H. Smith of Oregon lost his son, Garrett Lee, to suicide during his term in office. Thanks to Senator Smith's tireless advocacy, President George W. Bush signed the Garrett Lee Smith Memorial Act in 2004, authorizing $82 million for suicide prevention programs at colleges. Of great importance, but on a less public level, hundreds of support groups for suicide bereaved across the nation were started and are led by survivors of a loved one's suicide.

Certainly not all suicide bereaved will want to become involved in an endeavor related to suicide. The investment may be in something that was of special interest to the deceased loved one: sports, the infirm or elderly, the mentally or physically challenged, the homeless. It can be in something very low key and private, an endeavor as personal as making scrapbooks or photo albums for a generation that will never know the person who died. Some survivors make quilts or stuffed toys from the clothing of their family member. Others plant remembrance gardens or donate books to libraries or churches. Some write books or songs that tell of their journey toward healing to encourage newly bereaved. It matters not whether the tribute to the life of our beloved is big or small, public or private. It is the purpose and meaning that you, the survivor, find that holds the healing power.

We must transform the living relationship into loving memory. This may be the most difficult task of all. It is frightening and painful to relinquish attachment to the living relationship. Our intellect acknowledges the death as final long before our heart accepts that fact. We want and need to remember our loved one with clarity, with honesty, with love. Often to do so we must move from memories of events immediately preceding and following the death to memories of a happier, gentler, more loving past that we shared with the deceased. We may recall memories of a little boy with a bouquet of dandelions clutched in his fist, offering them to his mother; memories of a young father pitching a baseball to his son; of a teenage girl, proud and lovely in her first formal; of a wife happily preparing a holiday celebration for her family; a grandfather reading a story to a grandchild snuggled in his lap.

We will never forget how they died but at some point we must let the cause of death and memories surrounding it fade into the shadows and bring into the light, to sustain and accompany us into the future, treasured memories of how they lived and how their life enriched our own.

Taking Charge of Mourning

"A desire to be in charge of our own lives, a need for control,
is born in each of us. It is essential to our mental health,
and our success, that we take control."

U.S. Senator Robert Foster Bennett

Bewildering chaos reigns in the lives of those left behind in the days following the death of a loved one. Death by suicide magnifies the chaos. Emotions and their expression vacillate from disbelief to cries of anguish to expressions of rage to feelings of guilt and back to disbelief. Waves of grief batter us, sweeping us far away from the familiar, rolling us, sucking us under, spitting us out like rag dolls, limp, torn and disoriented. Our life is out of control; we can find nothing solid to cling to. It seems surreal. We feel totally helpless. We operate on automatic pilot. Nowhere feels safe.

Our sense of well-being is gradually restored as we use various means to help ourselves move from the helplessness of grief to taking charge or managing it, to begin restoring a bit of order and control in our life. Several survivors share their means of caring for themselves by managing their mourning: deciding what they need to move ahead and how to ask for what they need from others.

Melody works twelve hour shifts as a nurse. She took several weeks leave after her son ended his life. As she prepared to return to work, she dreaded the reactions of her colleagues, fearing their efforts to comfort her would destroy her composure and interfere with her work. Before returning to work, Melody sent her fellow nurses an e-mail stating her needs and expectations. She asked them not inquire about her well-being while she was on duty because doing so could trigger tears and shatter her professional stance. She gave them permission to speak of the manner of her son's death, say his name, and share remembered times with him during breaks. By stating her needs and expectations, Melody eased her way back to work as well as providing a comfort level for her co-workers.

Renee found work to be her salvation after her son's suicide. Her exacting work demanded total concentration. Returning to work the week following the funeral, Renee made herself focus for eight hours on her duties, to the exclusion of her grief. At the end of her work day, as soon as she got in the car to drive home, the tears came. Many times she had to pull over to the side of the road. Renee said the eight hours of respite from the outside world and from the torment of her loss was critical to her well-being. On the other hand, her husband, Chuck, tried to follow her example by returning to his work as manager of a legal office. He found his mind wandering and tears flowing; he felt that he was ineffective in his work. Chuck took a leave of absence and spent the time grieving in the safety of his home, regaining composure to enable him to provide productivity to his employer.

Vera's family was transferred to an overseas location when she and her brother, Barry, were in high school. After Barry ended his life during his high school junior year, Vera was concerned that speculation among members of their former community would destroy good memories of her brother. She wrote a brief letter that she sent to their former church to be printed in the church newsletter, to their school principal, and to close friends stating facts: "With deep sorrow I inform you my beloved brother, Barry Sheldon, died by his own hand on October 20, 2002, at age 17. Barry had been diagnosed with bipolar illness, was receiving treatment and counseling and we believed he was doing well. My father returned home from work to find Barry in the garage, dead by asphyxiation, with the car still running. We do not know why Barry ended his life. Barry's death leaves mother, dad and me in a world of pain and questions. Messages of comfort would be greatly appreciated. Our address is: _____ .

Sincerely, Vera Sheldon"

Jessica enrolled in a grief workshop several weeks after her father's suicide. Learning about grief in such an environment helped Jessica understand and embrace her pain and provided direction for managing her grief. Her progress caused the workshop director to enlist her as a leader of subsequent workshops. Jessica used what she learned in support of other suicide bereaved.

My husband returned to his office less than a week after our son's death. He welcomed the demand and distraction of responding to clients' needs. Because of his lengthy tenure in his position, he could effectively accomplish what needed doing almost automatically. Many male survivors return to work very soon following a significant other's death. For some it is a financial necessity. For others, the workplace is a familiar, safe, professional environment that contributes to maintaining composure.

I had not known that journaling was a practice recommended by grief counselors. As often as I talked with friends and family, talking was not enough to rid myself of the turmoil that roiled within me. During the early days of my acute grief I began to write. I found a partly used spiral notebook leftover from someone's school days, and I kept it close at hand. When my pain would boil over, as it constantly did, I would write and cry and write. Sometimes it was just a few words; sometimes it was pages. I could write about thoughts and feelings that I hadn't been able to talk about to those willing to listen. I would write healing bits of lyrics heard from the radio or television. I made notes of phrases I read or heard that soothed my pain. In the months following my son's death the notebook was filled, then misplaced and forgotten as I became involved in other ways of coping. About two years after my son's death I came across the dog-eared, tear-stained notebook and read what I had written early in my mourning. I wept for that mother, for her terrible hurt and need. There had been many sorrow-filled days when I questioned whether I was making any progress. The notebook offered me the assurance that, indeed, I had achieved a considerable measure of healing.

Whether we take charge of our mourning through counseling, attending grief workshops or support groups, or find other ways of moving forward, the responsibility is ours. Each tiny step by which we take control of our grieving process strengthens and reassures us that we can and will live through and beyond this tragedy. We are intended to grow through our grief to a level of mastery where we have conquered or gained control, are in charge—not "over it" or finished with pain and tears, not healed—but with control that enhances our sense of well-being. When we have moved beyond the depths of helplessness and despair to a plateau where we accept that what has happened cannot be changed, that we can and will live with the void created by the loss and, at some future juncture, find contentment and pleasure in life, then, my wounded friend, we are achieving what once seemed impossible. We are mastering our grief. We have been empowered with healing.

Victim ~ Survivor ~ Thriver

"... being a "survivor" does not mean that I have placed this event and its effects behind me. It means a willingness to continue to struggle with the past, to live in the present, and to be open to the future."

Maureen Stimming, *Before Their Time*

Family and friends are immobilized by horror, shock, and disbelief when a significant other ends his or her life. Their world they know has been shattered, leaving them confused, disoriented, without centering or grounding. They are thrust, protesting and unprepared, into the bewildering chaos of grief compounded by the self-inflicted death. They are powerless to ward off the vacillating feelings that sweep over them, sometimes including feelings of abandonment and rejection. Those left behind take a loved one's suicide very personally, for they have fallen victim to someone else's pain and the way that person resolved it.

In the preface to Albert Cain's book, *Survivors of Suicide*, Dr. Edwin Shneidman refers to suicide bereaved as survivor-victims. Julie, survivor of her father's suicide, personifies Dr. Shneidman's conclusion when she says, "I have been thrust into this vast, terrifying, confusion of grief because of my father's bad decision. I was not consulted. I was not given a choice. I wasn't even given an opportunity to help. I fell heir to his pain and problems . . . he left his suffering and hopelessness to me. I am a victim of his troubled mind, his desperation, his decision, his act."

In suicide's immediate aftermath it is not unusual for those left behind to fleetingly view themselves as victims. But the powerlessness of being a victim is debilitating, and to remain a victim is to accept a stagnant lifetime of grieving without healing, hope, or joy. To remain a victim is unhealthy and unnatural and deprives us of the strength to fight for survival.

Moving beyond being a victim is a choice we make. Often it is an unconscious choice instinctively made immediately following the death. We choose to survive. Surviving is defined as still living after another's death. But to achieve healthy survival we must reach out of our wounding to live the years that remain to us. Being forever mired in acute grief is intolerable. We struggle to regain our emotional balance, to cope with our loss, to accept both the death and the cause of the death. We fight for our life.

As victims, we may doubt our ability to live through the pain of the loved one's suicide, may even question whether or not we want to. But as survivors, we believe somehow we can, we will, and we do. Most survivors soon reject the label *victim*. They face the pain of grief and work hard to regain their emotional equilibrium. For a time, to make one breath follow another, one heartbeat follow another seems a herculean effort. Survivors scream, cry, and rage; they feel guilt and anger; they feel fear, doubt, and hopelessness. Their pain is beyond description. They long for a place where they won't hurt so badly. Some may think of the peace that would come with their own death. But the basic instinct is to live. And they do. They live knowing that causing their own death would place an insurmountable burden upon those left behind. Weary of the work of grief, the survivor longs for something beyond survival; something beyond the effort of breathing; something more than one heartbeat after another and mere existence. She/he longs for a vague, seemingly unattainable, place where life is pleasurable, peaceful, and fulfilling again.

As survivors suffer and struggle with the anguish of the loss, they grow. They grow emotionally stronger, grow in confidence, grow in knowledge and acceptance, grow to trust themselves and life again. They grow into thrivers.

Thriving is imperative to future happiness and well-being. Growing into a thriver does not mean the pain of the loss or its cause is gone, never to be felt again. Rather, it means the sharp, turbulent, obsessive, and constant anguish of acute grief has gentled into a tolerable, manageable feeling of profound sadness. The thriver may forever experience waves of grief but the raging tumult of acute grief is transformed. The once uncontrollable battering waves of emotional pain grow less frequent and fierce, eventually calming, smoothing, gentling into ripples of sorrow. The thriver recognizes feelings of guilt he once grappled with as deep regret that he couldn't prevent the death; regret for not having recognized and comforted the pain the loved one suffered; regret for things said or left unsaid, done or left undone; regret that he must live without that beloved person. The thriver recognizes he can and, perhaps always will, live with a measure of sorrow and regret. The thriver reconciles to the death and to its cause and knows that, although his life is forever changed, it is not over. The thriver is strengthened by understanding that this beloved person, and that person's death, is part of his own life, but it is not the whole of that life. Thrivers relinquish their bondage to suicide and grow toward a plateau where there is peace of mind, anticipation of the future, and feelings of joy. The thriver embraces life and lives again.

Newly bereaved reading these words may wipe their eyes, sigh deeply, and wish it could be so for them, not believing that they will survive, let alone thrive. Believe it, my wounded friend. There will be a time when you won't hurt as badly as you do today; a time when you will laugh without feeling guilty; a time when you will again experience pleasure and look forward to each day with gratitude. Yes, there is a time ahead when you will flourish, thrive.

A Peaceful Plateau

"To everything there is a season,
A time for every purpose under heaven:
A time to weep, and a time to laugh,
a time to mourn, and a time to dance."

Ecclesiastes 3:1, 4

In the throes of acute grief we are convinced there will never again be a time free of the pain of our loss or the burden of suicide; never a time when life is joyful again or when our entire being is not in turmoil. Peace is a state of existence free of conflict and strife. There is peace after the turbulent storm of grief subsides although it is not entirely free of emotional strife. Finding peace does not mean we never again feel pain for the loss of our loved one.

Finding peace after a loved one's suicide is achieved when the bereaved reconciles to the death and to the cause of death. Reconciling is coming to terms with what has occurred and arriving at a psychological/emotional acceptance that what has happened is fact that cannot be changed. Acceptance does not mean being in agreement. There will never be a time when we agree with what occurred.

To reach acceptance I have had to acknowledge that my son's death is and will forever be a mystery without satisfactory answer or conclusion. I will never know why. I have finally acknowledged that my future happiness does not depend upon having reasons or justification for his death and my loss. Acceptance is conceding that I must, that I can, and that I will live without my beloved child's physical presence for the remainder of my life.

A state of serene existence is not a plateau of absolute and constant happiness and joy. A state of serene existence is different for every mourner, just as what provides serenity differs. To me, peace or serenity comprises increments of contentment: minutes, hours, even days when I am free of sorrow and yearning. I find some peace from believing my son found the peace he sought, even though I don't like the way he went about it. I am at peace knowing I did the best I could with the knowledge I had at that time—and reaching that peace took a lot of time and soul-searching. I find peace in the assurance that all my surviving children have coped with their brother's death and its cause in as healthy a manner possible. Peace is trusting that my surviving family is going to be OK—different than I'd envisioned, but OK. My peace is enjoying moments of happiness and feeling joy again, experiences I once believed were forever gone from my life. Peace is thankfulness for what I had and gratitude for what remains to me. My most peaceful moments come from being with family and friends, driving in the mountains, working in the garden, talking to my children in heaven, and being given the strength to channel what I have experienced and learned into action that brings hope, enlightenment, and healing to others.

Yes, my wounded friend, there is peace ahead. It comes from doing the heart-heavy work of mourning, from knowing you are deserving of it, and from believing it is waiting for you to accept.

APPENDICES

Survivor Resources

<u>Alive Alone</u> offers support after the loss of an only child or all of one's children. *www.alivealone.org*

<u>American Association of Suicidology</u> (AAS) offers an annual healing day in conjunction with a national conference. *Surviving*, the AAS cyber newsletter, is available by subscription. AAS also publishes a Grief After Suicide Bibliography. Directory of suicide survivor support groups at *www.suicidology.org*

<u>American Foundation for Suicide Prevention</u> (AFSP) Walk Through Darkness commemorates suicide victims. AFSP also offers a Grief After Suicide Bibliography. Directory of suicide survivor groups at *www.afsp.org*.

<u>Center for Loss & Life Transition</u> offers suicide grief workbook, workshops, books. *www.centerforloss.com*

<u>HEARTBEAT Survivors After Suicide, Inc.</u> website, Words of Comfort, links to other support services and includes a guide for starting chapters. *www.heartbeatsurvivorsaftersuicide.org*

<u>Murder-Suicide Aftercare</u>, *Tawna@caascenter.org*

<u>Suicide Awareness\Voices of Education </u>(SA\VE) promotes suicide prevention through education. *www.save.org*

<u>Sibling Survivors</u> is a web site for siblings grieving a suicide loss. *www.siblingsurvivors.com*

<u>SOLOS-Partners</u> (SOLOS) offers support for romantic partners or spouses bereaved by suicide. *Solos-partners@yahoogroups.com*

<u>The Compassionate Friends</u> (TCF) is a national network of support groups addressing grief after the death of a child from any cause. *www.thecompassionatefriends.org*

The Dougy Center is a national organization for grieving children and families. *www.dougy.org*

Tragedy Assistance Program for Survivors (TAPS) offers support for the loved ones of those who served and died, with a support program specifically for survivors of military suicide. *www.taps.org*

Widow Net, *www.widownet.org*

To the Newly Bereaved After Suicide

Grieving is a unique, lonely, extremely painful process with all of us working through our own space at our own pace. It is comforting, however, to know what helped others who have experienced the anguish of a loved one's suicide.

"Give sorrow words. Grief has need to speak,
lest whisper the o'er fraught heart and bid it break."

Shakespeare, *Macbeth*, Act 4, Scene 3

Talk! Talk! Talk! Speak of your pain, your loss, and its cause as long and as often as you need to speak of it.

Be with your grief. Don't suppress, avoid, or postpone grief's expression. Let yourself feel the pain. Wail! Cry! Tears are cathartic and cleansing. Friends and extended family feel helpless faced with the magnitude of the loss and grief. They try to soothe, may even plead with bereaved not to cry. Don't suppress your grief to spare others distress. If you are reluctant to express your pain in others' presence, provide uninterrupted time each day to reflect upon the life shared, your loss and sorrow . . . a time to mourn. Take this private time during the day so you can allow yourself some pleasant distraction before you go to bed. In this manner you manage your grief and allow healing without imposing upon others.

Accept your friends' offers. . .to be with you, to share a meal, to run errands, to listen to your heartbreak. When you feel the times of being alone are unbearable, call upon them. Friends say, "Let me know how I can help." Most are sincere. By calling on friends when we need support, we allow them the gift of sharing our loss. On the other hand, if we continually refuse help, we may send the message that no help is needed and future offers would be an intrusion. Sensitive people will understand both your need for support and for time alone.

We seldom feel like accepting invitations, often for a long time, but consider going with close friends/family to small dinner parties, movies, concerts, sports events, and the like. So what if you lose your composure! These social events provide momentary respite from what has happened and are a useful focus when sleep is elusive or tormenting memories overwhelm us.

There is nothing funny about suicide or the death of someone we love but there is healing power in humor. It's OK to laugh. Laughter is healthy and healing. It releases chemicals that enhance one's sense of well-being. Laughter relaxes and rests us. It reassures our wounded psyche. Provide an opportunity for laughter by being with fun-loving people, watch a good comedy show, or rent a nonsensical movie. Don't expect films with a theme of violence, sex, or difficult social issues to be relaxing.

Re-establish routine in your life as soon as possible. People thrive on order in their lives, and a loved one's death disturbs it in the most devastating manner possible. Re-establishing routine is a major, necessary step in reminding us that life goes on and that we will regain well-being. For those who are confronted constantly by the family member's absence, re-establishing routine means redistribution of household chores and living arrangements. Adjusting to a loved one's death means many heartbreaking but necessary changes from life as it once was.

Acute grieving depletes energy, leaving little concern for good grooming. For a time it may take great effort and determination to shower, shave, arrange one's hair, and dress each morning, but caring for one's physical appearance is a critical step toward restoring well-being, balance, and order to one's life.

Provide the best opportunity for restful sleep by avoiding stimulants during the evening. Exercise is nature's antidepressant. Exercise enhances sleep opportunity. Caffeinated foods, including chocolate and some carbonated drinks, are sleep robbers. **Alcohol is a depressant** that magnifies an already depressed state of mind and does not contribute to restful, uninterrupted sleep. Alcohol masks feelings, lowers inhibition, and deprives one of control. Alcohol consumption should be avoided during acute grief.

Take the best possible care of yourself: your emotional being, your mental, spiritual, and physical being. Eat properly! Don't allow yourself to get too hungry or to go without meals. Try not to overeat. Often we experience a gnawing, empty feeling that we mistake as hunger and seek to fill that void with food that may be hard to digest or upsetting. Become informed of both the dynamics of grief and of suicide so that your grief is not unnecessarily complicated by myths, fears and biases. Pace yourself. This process is aptly called "grief work" and it is truly the most exhausting task your emotions, mind, and physical body will ever be called upon to do. You may experience some physical symptoms, for grief often manifests itself physically. Do not dismiss these symptoms; see your physician as soon as possible.

Grief and the workplace. For many bereaved it is an economic necessity to return to work soon after the funeral. Others return to work soon as a means of keeping mentally occupied and find solace in their work. Some postpone returning to their job fearing the additional stress created by work. Work can be helpful in restoring routine in one's life. Most employers are compassionate and sympathetic. Some have firsthand knowledge of loss and grief and extend encouragement and understanding. Others have a very unrealistic view of how long it takes to "get over" a family member's death and may not be tolerant of mistakes, distraction, or quick trips to the bathroom to dry tears. It can be helpful to discuss your limits and concerns with your employer, perhaps arriving at a compromise whereby you work a few hours a day when you first return to the job. It is also helpful when an employer engages a counselor to speak of suicide bereavement with fellow employees, placing them at greater ease in offering you support.

Suicidal thoughts are scary. When someone we love dies, we are overwhelmed by the pain of loss and fear of the future without them. We may believe we cannot endure the intensity of the pain. For a time, we may not wish to. When the cause of death is suicide, the surviving family members have been shown the worst possible example of how one can end pain and problems, and a survivor may view ending his/her life as a way to stop hurting. It is normal to want to escape the pain of loss and grief. It is not abnormal to think of ending one's own life to escape it. But there is considerable difference between having suicidal thoughts and acting upon them. If you are obsessed with thoughts of killing yourself, if you begin to think seriously about ways of ending your life or believe you don't deserve to live due to some circumstance surrounding the loved one's death, see a mental health professional without delay. It would be a grave injustice to compound the loss and magnify the grief of others by resolving your own feelings in this manner.

What's normal? What's not? Grief as we are taught to understand it is intensely distorted when suicide is the cause of death. You may question whether your feelings are normal. Most likely they are and you are experiencing normal emotional reactions to an abnormal occurrence, suicide. Grief after suicide is often effectively addressed within the safe environment of a suicide survivor support group. **Never hesitate to seek professional counseling.**

Posttraumatic Stress Disorder After Suicide

In defining emotional response to suicide, we recognize symptoms of posttraumatic stress. In the case of suicide survivors, rather than label the reactions as a "disorder," it seems more appropriate simply to call them a "normal reaction to an abnormal event" or, as Dr. Bob Boyle of the Englewood Trauma Treatment Center puts it, "too much, too fast, too ugly."

Sufferers of posttraumatic stress disorder are not crazy. They are reacting to an extremely traumatic experience. They feel pain, disorientation, and other emotions that seem so out of the ordinary they may fear they are losing their mind. It may be helpful for suicide survivors to know that the symptoms of posttraumatic stress are more severe when people are reacting to man-made disasters (war, assaults, imprisonment, torture, murder suicide) rather than natural disasters like floods, hurricanes, or tornadoes.

The symptoms of PTSD can show up immediately following the trauma or not for months or years. They can last a short while; they can last a lifetime. Because humans are good at denying or hiding feelings, especially when they are very painful, suicide survivors may experience nightmares that seem unrelated to the death of their loved one. These may occur soon after the suicide or much later. Hidden as the messages of these nightmares may be, they can be an indication that fear, anger, and guilt still need to be processed.

People Suffering Post Traumatic Stress May. . .

Re-experience the trauma in one of the following ways:

　　Recurrent recollection of the event

　　Dreams of the event

　　Obsession with what has happened

　　Suddenly feeling as if the event is recurring

Experience a numbing or reduced involvement with the world by:

    Lessening of interest in important activities; sense of purposelessness in existence

    Feeling detachment from other people and surroundings

    A flat, emotionless feeling

Have some of the following:

    Sleep disturbances

    Guilt about surviving

    Loss of memory, trouble concentrating

    Exaggerated startle response

    Avoidance of activities that arouse recollection of the trauma

    Distrust of self and others

    Identity confusion and isolation

    Hypervigilance

Both the severity and duration of the symptoms depend on how the survivors of suicide trauma are subsequently treated. Having to go it alone makes recovery from PTSD harder. Having no chance to talk about the experience makes it harder. Having no opportunity to understand what has happened and why it happened, not to mention guilt, stigma, and silence, all make it harder.

Putting Responsibility into Perspective

I have a responsibility TO those I love. . .

to be loving, patient, considerate and kind,

to be loyal, respectful and honest,

to be appreciative, encouraging and comforting,

to share myself and care for myself;

.....to be the best possible "ME".......

BUT

I am not responsible FOR them...

not for their achievements, successes or triumphs,

not for their joy, gratification or fulfillment,

not for their defeats, failures or disappointments,

not for their thoughts, choices or mistakes,

.....And, most of all, not for their suicide.......

For HAD I been responsible, this death would not have occurred.

To assume responsibility for this death, or to place responsibility upon another, robs the one who died of their personhood and invalidates the enormity of their pain and their desperate need to be free of it.

Heavy Hearts During Holidays*

Holidays can be difficult. Normally, they are a time for family fun and celebration, but when someone you love has died, the season may be painful and lonely.

When we are grieving, we feel completely overwhelmed with sadness. We miss the beloved person; we long for them. "How can I make it through these days?" we ask. "How will I survive?" Here are some ways of handling the holidays that have helped me to survive my losses. Maybe they can help you, too.

Your Body

Rest; you have experienced monumental loss. You are exhausted. Go to bed an hour earlier and nap frequently. Linger in the bathtub instead of taking a quick shower. Eat nourishing foods. Manage your sugar, caffeine, and alcohol intake; they affect mood. Drink water and green tea for energy restoration. Get a massage to remove toxins lodged deep within your muscles. Give and get as many hugs as you can; they do help console us. Walk briskly twenty minutes every day to elevate endorphins.

Your Mind

Begin a new tradition; the old ones could make you even sadder. If you ritually prepared an elaborate sit-down meal, take a break this year and go to someone else's home. If you don't have small children to attend to, simplify the decorations. An aromatic wreath on your front door, a manger, a menorah, a simple candle or figurine on the table surrounded by a little holly is more than enough.

Your Spirit

Offer it compassion; you did a good job loving the departed person and trust the heavens that they are now safe and free. Be around those people whom you love and who love you; their presence will soothe your weary soul. If you have a faith community, spend time with them for support. If not, consider finding one and go there to pray for peace, for faith, for grace, and for strength. Some of us who grieve find comfort praying at the grave site or reading a personal letter we composed or just speaking to the departed. Tears may come. Let them; they open up the gates for laughter and hope.

Each year, just after Thanksgiving, my husband and I place fresh wreaths by the memorials stones of our deceased children, our forever twenty-four-year-old son, Kent, who died by suicide in 1978 and our beautiful only daughter, Karen, who died of an illness in 2006 at age forty-nine. Stories of their humor and loving mischief often are recounted during gatherings with our remaining three sons and their families. This is a tender space for us all, where the veil between heaven and earth is thin. It is almost as though they are with us in person. I treasure these sacred times on a hundred levels.

Remember that your loved one's spirit never dies. If we can wrap our minds around that concept, a quiet shift will enter our souls and we will remember that the Creator of a million lifetimes will guide us in our next step. We will remember that our loved one is always with us as we are with them. And yes, we will remember and acknowledge that our life is not the same without them and we know that we will miss them forever and that no one can replace them.

But we are grateful, so very grateful, for having had the great blessing of them in our lives and their memory to treasure forever.

Part of this article was received as a photocopy without the author's name. It is so 'on the mark' I've chosen to provide it to survivors and hope the author will understand the solace it offers and forgive me for doing so.

Helping Survivors After Suicide

"The friend who can be silent with us in a moment of despair or confusion, who can stay with us in an hour of grief and bereavement, who can tolerate not knowing ~ not healing~ not curing ~ that is a friend who cares."

Henri Nouwen

The following suggestions are intended to guide you so that you can comfortably extend yourself to suicide bereaved without concern that you might do or say the wrong thing. The worst that can happen already has! You can't fix it, but you can comfort. The bereaved family benefits greatly from the consoling balm of love and shared sorrow from caring friends.

What can I say?

The most caring and honest words are "I am so sorry." You may wish to continue with "He/she will be missed" or even "I don't know what to say." If you were fond of the dead person or spent a fun or significant time with them, share that with the family. Every positive mention, every antic, amusing story, or reinforcing action involving the person who died is precious to the surviving family.

What can I do?

Be there. Anticipate and respond to need. Make sure water and tissues are at hand for the bereaved. A hug is appropriate and usually welcomed. However, there are those who do not wish to be touched, so you may choose to ask if you can give a hug. It is likely that you will shed tears in the presence of the newly bereaved, and that's OK, though it is best not to let crying get out of hand. Tears express deep empathy and knowing the death touches the hearts of others lends a bit of comfort and solace to the bereaved. It's helpful when someone maintains the kitchen, making refreshments available to callers, without displacing extended family members needing to help. Depending upon the situation, you may help by tending young surviving children, answering calls and recording callers, preparing meals,keeping records of gifts of flowers and food, doing yard or house work, making arrangements (e.g., funeral, travel, lodging), selecting and preparing funeral attire (laundry, cleaners) and, at a later time, writing thank you notes, helping file insurance or social security claims or seeking legal counsel.

The family may designate a spokesperson to address the cause and circumstance of the death with callers. Providing facts restores a measure of control to the immediate survivors and lessens opportunity for rumors and gossip. As much as possible, discourage secrecy regarding the cause of death. Secrecy severely distorts and complicates healthy grieving and can create family dissent and breaches. Increasingly, survivor families are openly designating contributions to suicide aftercare or suicide prevention organizations. Find whether there is a local support group for suicide bereaved, provide meeting information to the survivor, and offer to attend with them if this is permissible to the group leader. There are books and websites that provide support articles for suicide bereaved. A book or downloaded articles offers another avenue for validating their grief and assuring them they are not alone on this grief journey. If you know a long-term suicide survivor willing to extend empathy and reinforcement, ask the newly bereaved family if a call from the seasoned survivor would be helpful. In the weeks following the death, when all the tragedy-focused activity has subsided, the survivor needs calls, notes of support, dinner out (or brought in), visits, and distracting activities. Invitations may not be accepted, but the fact that they are extended is reinforcing.

Should I say the word 'suicide'?

If the cause of death is known or determined to be suicide, that's what it's called, and it's OK to say the word. Often "killed himself" or "ended her own life" is used, but there is really no soft, gentle way of saying *suicide*. I suggest *not* saying "committed suicide." *Committed* implies a crime. Suicide is not a crime. It is never appropriate to use crude phrases defining suicide.

Can I ask, "What happened?"

If you are a close friend or extended family member you may wish to say "Do you want to tell me what happened?"If you fear that question will be viewed as intrusive, be guided by what the bereaved is saying. Suicide is so shocking, traumatic, and usually unexpected that family members may have a need to talk about what took place, relating in detail the last word, actions, or what they found or saw. If you can't handle the details of the death, don't put yourself in a position to hear them. Don't tell the bereaved not to think or talk about the death or the circumstances surrounding the death. Talking is cathartic and a critical component in the grieving and healing process. You are there to support and help. Listening may be your most caring gift.

Should I say the deceased person's name?

There will never be a time when the family will not want to hear the name of the one who has died. Although the person is no longer living they are still a member of the family. Listening to the family will signal how you can talk about the death. When the family speaks of the deceased in the past tense, then the support community can do so as well.

Is it helpful to share faith-based views or past experience with suicide?

NO and NO. Please refrain from interpreting God's view on suicide. If the bereaved has questions regarding suicide in relationship to sin and religion, ask a clergy person to respond. It is not helpful to share judgmental beliefs about suicide nor, in the immediate aftermath, is it helpful or appropriate to share your personal struggles with mental illness, suicidal ideation, or attempts.

Are there topics to avoid?

It is never helpful to share the tragedies of others with newly bereaved persons. Don't try to cheer the bereaved person. There is a time for that, but the time is not in the days following the death. Be as natural and positive as possible. Deflect statements that perpetuate bias and misconception around the issue of suicide.

How long before the bereaved are healed and back to normal?

Adjusting to the loss of someone dearly loved is a life work in progress. Grief is not time-limited or measurable. Like a snowflake, grief is unique, with each individual coping in their own space at their own pace. The old normal is gone; a new normal will evolve. The lives of the surviving family are forever changed by this tragedy but eventually the initial raging grief gentles into sorrow and regret that's tolerable and manageable. Be alert for indications of obsessive guilt, anger, or talk of wanting to die. While it is not unusual or abnormal for suicide bereaved to speak of not wanting to live, it can also be a red flag. If such talk persists, for the safety of the bereaved and peace of mind of those who care for them, encourage an immediate appointment with a mental health professional.

A Suicide Survivor's Beatitudes

LaRita Archibald

BLESSED are they who recognize suicide grief is compounded; that we grieve the death of a beloved person, but first and foremost we grieve the cause of the death.

BLESSED are they who give us permission to mourn the loss of one dearly loved, free of judgment, censure and shame.

BLESSED are spiritual guides who relieve our concerns for the repose of our loved one's soul with the truth that God is all-knowing, all-loving, and all-forgiving.

BLESSED are they who don't offer the meaningless cliché "time heals," because for a long while the passing of time holds no meaning or value for us.

BLESSED are they who don't say, "I know just how you feel," but instead say, "I am here for you. I will not tire of your tears or your words of sorrow and regret."

BLESSED are they who have the patience and love to listen to our repetitive obsession with Why? . . . without offering useless answers or explanations.

BLESSED are they who reaffirm the worth of our deceased beloved by sharing memories of his/her goodness and times of fun, laughter, and happiness.

BLESSED are mental health care providers who explain to us that, very probably, our loved one died of a terminal illness called depression.

BLESSED are they who challenge our sense of omnipotence with the reminder that no one has enough power or control over another to cause them to end their life.

BLESSED are first responders to our loved one's suicide who try to relieve our sense of guilt and responsibility by assuring us "This death is not your fault."

BLESSED are they who lend acceptance to the value of the relationship we shared with the one who died by allowing us to speak of them and "what might have been. "

BLESSED are they who allow and encourage us to use our loved one's death in a manner that gives our loss and grief meaning and purpose.

BLESSED are they who do not expect us to find "closure," "grief resolution," "recovery" or to "be healed," understanding that these terms define grief work in progress that will take the rest of our life.

BLESSED are community caregivers who direct us to suicide bereavement support groups where our anguish is understood, our loss validated, and where we are encouraged by the example of others who have traveled this road before us.

BLESSED are seasoned suicide survivors, role models, who show us not only that we can survive, but, in time, we will thrive...we will regain peace of mind, confidence, productivity and zest for living.

BLESSED are all who honor our loved ones by remembering how they lived rather than how they died.

Made in the USA
Charleston, SC
20 October 2012